Homeric Hymns

Homeric Hymns

Translated by Sarah Ruden

Introduction and Notes by Sheila Murnaghan

Hackett Publishing Company, Inc.
Indianapolis/Cambridge

11 10 09   2 3 4 5 6 7

For further information, please address:
Hackett Publishing Company, Inc.
P. O. Box 44937
Indianapolis, Indiana 46244–0937

www.hackettpublishing.com

Cover design by Abigail Coyle and Brian Rak

Text design by Meera Dash

Composition by William Hartman

Printed at Victor Graphics, Inc.

Library of Congress Cataloging-in-Publication Data

Homeric hymns. English.
    Homeric hymns / translated by Sarah Ruden ; introduction and
notes by Sheila Murnaghan.
        p. cm.
    Translation of 34 ancient Greek poems.
    Includes bibliographical references (p.   ).
    ISBN 0-87220-726-9 (cloth) — ISBN 0-87220-725-0 (pbk.)
    1. Homeric hymns—Translations into English.   2. Hymns, Greek
(Classical)—Translations into English.   3. Gods, Greek—Poetry.
I. Ruden, Sarah.   II. Title.

    PA4025.H8R83 2005
    883'.01—dc22
                                                    2005012991
        ISBN-13: 978-0-87220-726-4 (cloth)
        ISBN-13: 978-0-87220-725-7 (pbk.)

Contents

Introduction

In the *Homeric Hymns,* we see the ancient Greeks reaching out through song to the individual gods who made up their pantheon. The thirty-four poems vary in length and date of composition, but each is designed to win a god's favor by naming and celebrating his or her particular powers. The briefer hymns invoke their subjects through a few key attributes, but the longest and most impressive ones tell fully-developed stories about how a god's powers were either first acquired or decisively affirmed. These stories are defining episodes in the evolution of the cosmos: each explains features of the world order that governs the lives of gods and humans alike—marriage, death, agriculture, religious worship, prophecy, music.

The title "Hymn," by which these poems are known, derives from the Greek word *humnos,* which originally meant simply "song" and thus referred to all forms of poetry, since poetry was always sung in one way or another throughout most of Greek history. Only later, perhaps in the fourth century BCE, did *humnos* come to mean a song in honor of a god. The *Homeric Hymns* clearly fit this more restricted later definition. However, they are also closely related to the other songs that belong, as most of the *Hymns* themselves do, to the earliest phase of Greek literature, the period around 750–700 BCE, when the Greeks acquired the art of writing and used it to preserve the traditional poetry that had been handed down through oral performance: the two epics that are also attributed to Homer, the *Iliad* and the *Odyssey,* and two poems by Hesiod, the *Theogony* and the *Works and Days.* All of these are instances of solo song, as opposed to the choral songs performed by groups of singers who also danced, that we hear of within those works and know from later examples. Solo songs were performed by individual singers, who accompanied themselves on the lyre. The *Hymns* share with these other early instances of solo song a focus on narrative, a particular meter,

the dactylic hexameter, and a particular style, which includes fre-
quent repetition of familiar phrases, such as combinations of
names and epithets (for example, "Zeus the counselor" or
"lovely-haired Demeter"). This style reflects the common origin
of these works in a tradition of oral poetry in which such phrases
are an indispensable aid to extemporaneous composition. From
what we can tell, the singing involved was a form of heightened
recitation, more musical than ordinary speech, but not full-
fledged melodic song.

In addition, the *Hymns*, the Homeric epics, and the poems of
Hesiod all draw on a common mythological tradition that
explains the interconnected circumstances of gods and humans.
The *Iliad* and the *Odyssey* may focus on human characters, but
those characters' lives are shaped by the same gods who are the
main subjects of the *Homeric Hymns*, and their stories cannot be
told until the poet has called on a powerful divinity, the Muse,
for help. As the *Hymns* reveal, the powers and activities of the
gods acquire their meaning through their effects on mortals,
even if mortals play only supporting roles in the stories told.
These poems assume a common universe populated by many
divinities, all related to each other in a complex genealogical
scheme. At its center is a group of gods known as the Olympians,
because they live on Mount Olympus, who form an extended
family dominated by the most powerful god of all, the sky-god
Zeus. Zeus's rule is endless—it is destined to last forever—but it
has not always existed. Zeus has had to struggle to come to
power, and his supremacy has a history, of which the stories told
in the *Homeric Hymns* form some of the final chapters.

Our main source for the earlier chapters of this history is
Hesiod's *Theogony* or "Origins of the Gods." The *Theogony* tells
how hundreds of Greek gods, Olympian and non-Olympian,
came into existence over a period of several generations, during
which supreme power passed from father to son in a series of
violent conflicts. In the first such episode, Zeus's father Cronus
defeats his own father (and Zeus's grandfather) Uranus by cas-
trating him with a giant sickle. In the next generation, Zeus
defeats his father and the other gods of his father's generation,

the Titans, in a huge battle. But Zeus's greatest accomplishment is that he is able to avoid the fate of his father and grandfather and acquires permanent power. He does this by forestalling the catastrophe that overtakes both of his predecessors: defeat by a son who is stronger than his father.

Zeus learns that his consort Metis (whose name means "cunning intelligence" or "clever planning") is destined to give birth first to a daughter and then to a son who will surpass his father. While she is still pregnant with the first of these destined children, he contrives to swallow her. Having incorporated Metis within himself, he gives birth to his daughter, the clever warrior goddess Athena, who springs into the world from Zeus's head. Through this maneuver, Zeus at once prevents the birth of a son who could usurp him and provides himself with a much more satisfactory offspring, a child who resembles her father in intelligence and strength but who, being female, cannot compete with him. Athena is not only a warrior but a perennial virgin, a loyal daughter who will never leave her father's side and acquire the unsettling new attachments to husband and children that come with marriage. In swallowing Metis, Zeus overcomes the unpredictable challenge of female fertility, appropriating for himself and bringing under control the ability to bring forth new creatures.

Outdoing his father and grandfather in this way, Zeus at once reveals his superiority among the gods and reaffirms the difference from human beings that makes the gods divine. It is humans who are subject to the process of generational succession, through which sons inevitably grow stronger than their fathers and replace them, and who have to engage in sexual reproduction, entangling themselves with women and giving away their daughters in marriage so that the race can continue. The glory of Zeus's rule is its stability, and with his ascent to power the divine universe stops evolving. From then on, it is only the humans who have to endure and cope with the losses and dislocations brought by change.

Zeus shores up the stability of his rule through a process of power sharing by which he grants prerogatives, or spheres of influence, to the other members of his family, the siblings and offspring who might otherwise rebel against him. In the *Theogony*, Hesiod recounts that, after the battle with the Titans, the other Olympians urged Zeus to be their king and he "distributed their honors among them" (*Theogony* 885). How Zeus came to terms with the other Olympians is one of the recurrent themes of Greek mythology and a natural subject for the *Homeric Hymns*, which focus on individual gods and their claims.

The *Hymns* record episodes from this dynamic final phase of divine history, when the relations among the Olympians are still being settled. There we get, especially in the four longest hymns (to Demeter, Apollo, Hermes, and Aphrodite [2–5]), a series of narratives in which the birth or self-assertion of a particular Olympian god presents Zeus with a crisis that has to be resolved; as the plot moves toward a resolution, the issues raised in the story of Zeus's initial assumption of power return and have to be addressed once again. Thus several of the *Hymns* deal with the lurking threat of the more powerful offspring, including a brief hymn dedicated to Athena. In the *Hymn to Athena* (28), we see what an alarming event the birth of a new god can be. As she leaps fully-armed from Zeus's head, the gods are seized with awe, Olympus spins in fright, the earth screeches, the sea froths, and the sun stands still. But in a brief moment, the crisis is over. Athena takes off her armor, demonstrating her amiability and showing herself to be female: "This was Pallas Athena, joy of wise Zeus" (*Hymns* 28.16).

The longer *Hymn to Apollo* (3) deals with the more substantial threat of the birth of Zeus's most powerful son. The poem opens again with the dangerous moment of the new god's arrival on Olympus, in a description that seems to evoke both Apollo's first appearance among the Olympians and his every appearance there: "All gods but one rise quickly from their seats, / All but one shake while he is striding toward them / Through Zeus's house, drawing his glittering bow" (3.2–4). The one who is not afraid is Apollo's mother Leto, who disarms her son much as the motherless Athena has disarmed herself. Leto removes Apollo's bow from his shoulder and hangs it on a peg. Zeus gladly welcomes his son with a cup of nectar, and "The gods around them / Can now sit down" (3.11–12). This is followed by an account of Apollo's birth that develops the same conception of Apollo as capable of threatening his father and with him the order of the universe, but choosing not to.

The first half of the *Hymn to Apollo* (3) tells how hard it was for Leto to find a place where she could give birth to Apollo. We are given a long catalog of places that refused her out of fear of Apollo's immense force. The problem is voiced by Delos, the rocky island that is Leto's last resort (which figures in the narrative as at once a place and its personified goddess). "They say Apollo in his arrogance / Will lord it over everyone—immortals, / And mortal men as well on fields where wheat grows" (3.67–69). Delos agrees, however, because she is so poor that she needs the rich offerings that will be brought by worshipers to Apollo's birthplace. Apollo's birth on Delos is a momentous event, attended by many goddesses, and he is a prodigious child, quickly bursting out of the golden swaddling clothes in which his divine nurses attempt to bind him. But once he speaks his first words, it is clear that all is well. "Apollo spoke among the deathless women: / 'I will be patron of the lyre and curved bow, / And prophet of the changeless will of Zeus'" (3.130–132). Apollo claims powerful prerogatives for himself, important instruments of warfare and civilization and the essential function of prophecy, but also asserts that he will not challenge his father: instead he will serve his father as the chief interpreter to mortals of his father's will, which he acknowledges as invincible. In this version of the story, Apollo himself forestalls any need for Zeus to negotiate with him, proposing an acceptable settlement from the outset. The second half of the *Hymn* describes how Apollo, with Zeus's blessing, establishes his oracle at Delphi.

The *Hymn to Hermes* (4) tells how the equilibrium achieved through the honors granted to Apollo is unsettled by the birth of yet another son of Zeus with ambitions of his own. Hermes is the child of Zeus and a less formidable mother than Leto, the mountain nymph Maia. The instant he is born, Hermes recognizes himself as the disadvantaged younger son, who must compete

with his established, favored older brother. He loses no time seiz-
ing a herd of cattle belonging to Apollo, staking a claim both to a
share of Apollo's prizes and to his own distinctive sphere of influ-
ence—trickery and theft. While still a baby, Hermes sneaks out of
the cave where he lives with his mother and leads off and hides
the cattle. When Apollo descends in rage on Hermes, now back
in his cradle and vigorously denying everything, a terrible stand-
off ensues, until they refer the matter to Zeus. Zeus both delights
in and sees through Hermes's lies and sends him off to guide
Apollo to the cattle. In this way, Zeus acknowledges both of his
sons, affirming Apollo's truthfulness and right to the cattle but
also assigning Hermes one of his enduring functions, that of
guide. At Zeus's direction, Apollo and Hermes work out their
differences in a complex transaction. Hermes does have to return
Apollo's cattle, but that does not mean he ends up with nothing.
At the seeming moment of defeat, he plays his trump card, show-
ing off a dazzling invention that Apollo cannot do without.

On his way to steal the cattle, Hermes has encountered a tor-
toise at the door of his mother's cave. He speaks to the tortoise
with ingratiating words, then grabs and kills her, scoops out her
shell, and turns the shell into a lyre, inventing a wonderful toy
for himself. When he later pulls out the lyre and starts playing
with it, Apollo is enthralled and must have it. Hermes's inven-
tiveness thus gives him the bargaining power he needs to gain
something from Apollo. The lyre is traded for a whip, and Her-
mes becomes the god of herding. In addition, Apollo gives him
an odd little oracle of his own, one that involves prophetic bee-
women. Apollo and Hermes become fast friends, and the dis-
ruptive potential of sibling rivalry is neutralized. This outcome
depends on a differentiation of functions, through which the
family relations among the gods become a way of articulating
the relationships between activities and concepts. The older and
younger brothers stand for the distinctions to be drawn
between Apollo's attributes of truthfulness, open warfare, sta-
bility, order, and light, and Hermes's attributes of deception,
theft, mobility, and shady nocturnal doings. At the same time,
the intimate transactions among the brothers reveal that these

attributes cannot be wholly differentiated. The lyre with which Apollo establishes the rhythms of civilization depends, as it turns out, on Hermes's inventiveness and cold-blooded exploitation of the tortoise.

In the two other longer hymns, which honor Demeter and Aphrodite (2 and 5, respectively), Zeus is forced to contend with the power of female divinities. In negotiating the births of his children, Zeus manages to dodge the dangers associated with female fertility, whether by absorbing Metis into himself or by relying on the gracious self-subordination of Leto. But he confronts fertility once again in his dealings with Demeter, who is both his sister and the mother of his daughter Persephone. Demeter is at first a casualty of Zeus's need to share power with his two brothers, Poseidon and Hades. Various myths allude to the fact that Zeus and his two brothers divided up the universe among them, in some versions by lot, in others by common agreement. In this division, Zeus gains control over the sky, Poseidon over the sea, and Hades over the underworld.

The story of Demeter and Persephone stems from the concession Zeus must make to Hades to compensate him for drawing a gloomy kingdom devoid of inhabitants, which is that Zeus gives Hades Persephone as a wife. When Hades snatches Persephone up from the meadow where she is picking flowers and drags her down to the underworld, he both gains a companion for himself and traces the route by which all of the people of the earth will eventually travel to his realm and become his subjects. In making what seems to be a satisfactory arrangement among the male gods of his generation, Zeus overlooks Demeter and the power of fertility that she represents. Demeter responds to the loss of her daughter with an overwhelming rage that sends her on a series of adventures and eventually leads her to suspend the fertility of the earth. As a result, humans wither and die and can no longer provide the gods with the rich sacrifices they require. This creates a crisis that Zeus cannot ignore, and he must negotiate with Demeter, revising his arrangement with Hades to accommodate her. Persephone no longer belongs only to Hades, but spends two-thirds of every year with her mother.

With Aphrodite, however, Zeus is able to assert a clear upper hand, as he is not with Demeter and, far from bowing to her power, he makes her weaker. Aphrodite is his daughter, not his sister, and she represents the less respectable female power of sexual seductiveness. In the different fates of Demeter and Aphrodite, we see again how the divine pantheon can function as a means of comparing and distinguishing various attributes. Nowhere in the *Hymn to Demeter* (2) do we hear of the sexual relations between Zeus and Demeter that led to the birth of Persephone. Demeter appears only as a mother and the divine patron of the earth's productiveness. Sexuality is confined to Aphrodite, who is taken far less seriously.

The *Hymn to Aphrodite* (5) acknowledges Aphrodite's power and portrays it in memorable ways but also stresses the limits of that power. The poem opens by naming three revered virgin goddesses who are unaffected by Aphrodite: Athena; Artemis, Apollo's sister and goddess of hunting and wild animals; and Hestia, goddess of the hearth. It then goes on to tell a story about how Zeus gets the better of Aphrodite. Fed up with Aphrodite's ability to humiliate male gods by making them fall in love with mortal women, and then laughing about it, Zeus punishes her by turning her power on herself and making her fall in love with a mortal man, Anchises, whom she then sets out to seduce. By the end of the hymn, Aphrodite is no longer in a position to make fun of the other gods for their susceptibility to mortals. And it appears, although the poem doesn't quite say this, that the series of matings between gods and mortals that produced great heroes, like Aeneas, the son Aphrodite will bear to Anchises, have come to an end. In this way, too, Zeus's arrangements lead to greater stability and a clearer distinction between gods and mortals.

Each of the stories told in the longer *Homeric Hymns* resolves a particular crisis and settles the question of how a particular god fits into the Olympian order, sharpening the definition of Zeus's rule. But these are not the only stories of this kind that could be told or were told (just as these thirty-four surviving hymns were by no means the only poems of their kind composed in antiquity), and the threats Zeus masters in these episodes are never entirely put to rest. Throughout Greek mythology, Zeus is always subject to challenges from within his family, in particular from his wife Hera, who confronts him over and over again with rebellious assertions of female power. Of the many goddesses with whom Zeus mates, Hera is the one who is officially his wife, and this makes her perennially jealous of all his other lovers.

Hera's jealousy is a constant theme of mythology and figures a number of times in the *Homeric Hymns,* especially in the *Hymn to Apollo* (3). Offended by Leto's impending motherhood, Hera keeps Eileithyia, the indispensable goddess of childbirth, on Olympus until the other goddesses manage to lure her away. After he is born, Apollo shows his allegiance to his father by killing the monster Typhaon, whom Hera produced on her own in a resentful response to Zeus's solo production of Athena. In another story, alluded to in the fragmentary *Hymn to Dionysus* (1) that begins the collection, Hera takes vengeance on Dionysus's mother Semele by getting her to ask her lover Zeus to visit her in his true form. He has no choice but to come as the thunderbolt, and Semele burns to death, but Zeus snatches up the unborn Dionysus and sews him into his own thigh, from which Dionysus is born when his gestation is complete. Once again, Zeus circumvents the ongoing challenge posed by Hera and again demonstrates his own capacity to give birth. Zeus's mastery is never really in doubt, but it must be asserted over and over again.

Although the Olympian gods may strike modern readers as astonishingly similar to human beings, their differences from mortals are essential to their identities, and the *Hymns* reinforce those identities by defining and redefining the boundaries between the divine and the human. In some episodes, the gods enter closely into human experience, only to draw back and reassert their divinity. In other episodes, humans approach the divine, only to have their mortal limits reaffirmed. The roguish latecomer Hermes is the Olympian who is most in danger of slipping into mortality. Like a mortal, he has a fully imagined body, with all its biological functions and alterations through

time. Unlike Apollo, Hermes has a real babyhood, complete
with cradle and swaddling clothes, and Hermes is the god who
farts and sneezes. In the story of Hermes's self-realization, there
is a moment of crisis when he slaughters two of Apollo's cattle
and experiences a powerful desire to eat their meat. Eating real
food, as opposed to nectar and ambrosia, is a mark of humanity.
Only humans have to repair the effects of time by nourishing
themselves; their need for food binds humans to constant labor,
something of which the gods are happily ignorant. When Her-
mes overcomes his craving for meat, he proves that he belongs
where he thinks he does, among the Olympians.

Along the same lines, Zeus's vengeance on Aphrodite takes
the form of entangling her with human beings. Just as Aphrodite
has confused the natural hierarchy by making male gods tempo-
rarily subject to the mortal women they desire, so she loses the
upper hand through her own humiliating desire for Anchises.
For her, however, the humiliation is lasting because she becomes
pregnant with a son, who will bind her permanently to mortality.
As she sums it up on the morning after, "I went crazy— / Terri-
bly: left my mind somewhere behind me, / Slept with a man—
beneath my belt's a baby" (5.253–255). She names her baby
"Aeneas," after a Greek word for "grievous," "for my anguish /
In stumbling into bed with you, a mortal" (5.198–199). It is as
the parents of mortals who must suffer and die that the gods
come closest to feeling the pain that is the common lot of all
human beings (a theme familiar to readers of the *Iliad,* which
records the grief of Achilles's divine mother Thetis over his fate).

In the *Hymn to Demeter* (2), both Persephone and Demeter
experience versions of mortality. As she is abruptly snatched
away from her friends and plunged into a new world, Perse-
phone is like a mortal woman entering into marriage, which the
Greeks often compared to death, and her journey to the under-
world prefigures the similar journey that will be taken by count-
less mortals after her. Her permanent consignment to the
underworld for one-third of each year is sealed when she eats a
pomegranate seed presented to her by Hades. This assimilates
her to mortals both because eating is what mortals do, and

because the act of taking in her husband's seed suggests sexual intercourse, on which mortals must rely for the continuation of their race.

Like a human mourner, Demeter responds to Persephone's abduction by imitating the deathly state of the one who is lost. In her case, that means not only tearing her clothes and fasting, but also leaving Olympus behind and entering the realm of mortals, where she assumes the identity of a powerless and timeworn old woman. Going to the town of Eleusis, Demeter is welcomed by the royal family and enters their household as a humble nurse. There she embarks on what appears to be an attempt to make up for Persephone's loss by abducting another child, trying to turn her charge, the royal heir Demophoön, into a god by secretly placing him in the fire at night. This project comes to an abrupt end when Demophoön's mother Metaneira sees what Demeter is doing and cries out in fright. This enrages Demeter, who recovers her divine identity, puts the baby on the ground, denounces Metaneira for her stupidity, and stalks off to adopt the far more successful and godlike strategy of suspending the whole earth's fertility.

The Demophoön episode reasserts the uncrossable boundary between mortals and immortals. As the child of an ordinary, worried human mother like Metaneira, Demophoön could never really have become a god. This same barrier is sadly contemplated by Aphrodite as she muses on her attraction to Anchises, knowing he will one day be wrapped in old age, something no god can bear to see. Only Zeus, it seems, has been successful in adopting a human, the Trojan boy Ganymede, and even Ganymede remains in a subordinate position, as Zeus's cupbearer. The hymns envision moments of intimacy between gods and humans, but those moments can never last. Aphrodite and Anchises jump into bed with equal eagerness, but the next morning she's suddenly towering over him while he begs her not to punish him for the terrible transgression of sleeping with a goddess. Metaneira welcomes Demeter to her house with words of sympathy for her ancient, downtrodden state: "The bitter gifts of gods are ours to suffer. / Their yoke lies on our

necks. Since you have come here, / Whatever I myself have, you
may have it" (2.216–218); but soon afterward Metaneira is her-
self suffering the goddess' bitter wrath as Demeter upbraids her
for her all-too-human unawareness.

The gap in understanding between Demeter and Metaneira is
one example of the remarkable play of perspectives found
throughout the *Hymns*. What to Metaneira is a natural expres-
sion of maternal concern as she sees her beloved baby in the fire
is to Demeter an intolerable sign of mortal shortsightedness.
The *Hymn to Hermes* (4) captures the different views of older
son and younger son in Apollo's impatience with "this thieving
little thug" (4.336) and Hermes's determination as he tells his
mother, "We're not just staying here . . . in this dank cave"
(4.168–172).

The *Hymn to Demeter* (2) is notable for foregrounding female
perspectives on events that belong to a patriarchal world order.
Not only does the plot tell how that patriarchal order is forced to
modify itself in recognition of female power, but the narrative
focuses on the subjective experiences of the female characters:
Persephone clinging to hope as the familiar world recedes from
view; Demeter clutched by sharp pain as she hears her daughter's
inexplicable cry; the shared joy of mother and daughter when
they are finally reunited. The poem stresses the ways in which
women reach out to one another, as when Hecate helps Deme-
ter discover what has happened to Persephone, or when Meta-
neira invites Demeter into her house. It depicts several groups of
women united by shared pleasures: the nymphs who pick flowers
with Persephone, the heiferlike daughters of Celeus, the god-
desses who join Demeter in celebrating Persephone's return. At
the same time, the hymn is sensitive to the differences between
mother and daughter, who may not view Persephone's marriage
as equally tragic; questioned by her mother, Persephone is oddly
defensive about the pomegranate seed that binds her perma-
nently to Hades.

The *Hymn to Aphrodite* (5) easily combines several attitudes
to Aphrodite. The poem recounts how she is rightly punished by
Zeus for taunting and tormenting him and the other gods, but it

also celebrates her dazzling charms: her heavenly sweet perfume; her irresistible effect on the wild animals who turn to mating as she rushes past; the pins, spiral brooches, necklaces, earrings, and shining belt taken off by Anchises as he, "A man, badly informed, slept with a goddess" (5.167).

Even as the gods define themselves by insisting on their distance from mortals, they also bring great benefits to mortals; not all gifts of the gods are bitter. Carving out their spheres of influence, the gods define features of existence that humans also can enjoy, like Apollo's music and Aphrodite's lovemaking. In the process of staking his claim to a place on Olympus, Hermes comes up with numerous valuable inventions: the lyre, sandals, fire sticks, and the pan-pipe. Some of the gods' gifts are designed to compensate in some degree for the gulf that separates them from mortals. Not only does Apollo benefit the inhabitants of Delphi when he establishes his oracle, ridding them of a terrible monster and providing them with a source of revenue through the visitors who will be drawn there, but the oracle itself is a means by which all humans can gain knowledge of the otherwise inaccessible mind of Zeus. Demeter helps the Eleusinians, who cannot hope to see through her disguises and interact successfully with her in person, by providing them with a cult through which they can, through regular observance, secure her favor.

The resolution of Demeter's story involves divine mitigation of the human condition on many levels. Insofar as Persephone's experience represents mortality, her consignment to the underworld is not absolute, but is relieved by her annual visits to Olympus. When Persephone is released from constant death, Demeter restores the fertility of the earth, through which mortals are able to feed themselves and keep death temporarily at bay. Persephone's annual movements bring the seasons, which enables the orderly cultivation of the earth. Demophoön may be consigned once again to mortality when Demeter puts him down on the earth, but he (like Anchises' son Aeneas) has gained the status of a hero, which is the closest mortals ever get to immortality. "But since I held him sleeping on my lap, / He will possess lifelong, unwithering honor" (2.263–264). And the cult established by Demeter in Eleusis, the Eleusinian Mysteries, offers anyone who is initiated into it a better experience after death. Because of its secret nature, we don't know exactly what happened during initiation into the Mysteries, but it seems clear that initiates partly reenacted the experiences of Demeter as told in this hymn. Some of the details of her behavior in the house of Celeus, such as sitting on a stool covered with a sheepskin, drinking a special drink, and hearing bawdy jokes, correspond to details of Eleusinian ritual. Her joyous reunion with Persephone evidently prefigures the final revelation of the Mysteries and the happier afterlife that initiates can look forward to. No wonder that the poem ends with praise of Persephone and Demeter: "Happy among the earthbound / Is anyone who feels their love and kindness" (2.486–487). Like the other hymns, the *Hymn to Demeter* (2) expresses veneration by spelling out both the gods' awesome superiority to earthbound mortals and their generous favor.

Among the greatest of the pleasures that the gods share with mortals is music. We hear of several musical occasions in the *Hymns,* of which the finest are the gatherings on Olympus described in the *Hymn to Apollo* (3), where Apollo plays his lyre and leads the other gods in dancing, while the Muses remind them of the glory of immortality: they "Sing of the gods' eternal gifts, the hardships / Of humans at the hands of the immortals, / Our mindless, helpless lives that never find / A cure for death, a guard against old age" (3.190–193). But even helpless mortals have godlike moments, and these include festivals, like the festival in honor of Apollo on Delos, described in the same *Hymn.* There all the Ionian Greeks gather and honor the god with competitions in boxing, dancing, and the work of singers. "Whoever sees this people all together / Would say that they were ageless and immortal" (3.151–152).

This account of the great annual gathering on Delos, with its poetic competitions in honor of Apollo, provides one possible context for the original performances of the *Homeric Hymns.* Another, less formal setting is suggested by the description of what Hermes did with his new lyre: "He sang along quite nicely— / Improvisations such as young boys warble / When at some festival they taunt each other" (4.54–56). It is possible, but not certain, that the *Hymn to Demeter* (2) was performed at Eleusis, in connection with the celebration of the Mysteries. Yet another possibility is suggested by the episode in the eighth book of Homer's *Odyssey* in which a bard attached to the court of a great king performs at a banquet, singing a song about Ares and Aphrodite that is similar to the *Homeric Hymns*.

These possibilities place the *Hymns* in a range of settings, similar to those in which we believe the Homeric epics took shape. While some may strike us as more obviously religious than others, all musical performances were understood by the Greeks as inspired by the gods and carried out in their honor, as were other displays of human excellence, such as the boxing matches conducted by the Ionians on Delos. Songs on all occasions required the sponsorship of the Muses, whose own singing and dancing on Olympus was the prototype for all mortal performances. Songs were not segregated by subject matter, and singers moved easily between divine and human topics. This is illustrated by the Delian women whose songs are praised in the *Hymn to Apollo* (3): "The girls who sing, to start, about Apollo, / Next Leto and her arrow-pouring daughter; / They call to mind then all the men and women / Of the time gone, to charm the gathered nations" (3.158–161). This close connection is also suggested by some of our ancient sources, which identify the *Hymns* as *prooimia*, or "prologues" to other narratives like the *Iliad* and the *Odyssey*. This identification is by no means certain, but not unlikely, at least in the case of the shorter *Hymns*, especially since a number of them end with the promise of another song. Hesiod's *Theogony* begins with what is essentially a hymn to the Muses, giving the story of their birth and describing their arrival on Olympus. The *Hymns* stand apart from these other poems as a separate genre only because of the way they are addressed to individual gods, and their distinctive structure.

The typical structure of the *Hymns* involves a characteristic beginning and ending. They open by establishing a connection with the god in question; this is accomplished first by naming him or her and then by listing the god's attributes and places of worship. They end with a final salute, a request for the god's favor (sometimes in the form of victory in the contest in which the hymn is performed), and sometimes the announcement that another song will follow. So one of the shorter hymns to Aphrodite (6) ends, "Joy, sexy-glancing darling. In this contest, / Give me the victory. Make my hymn ready— / The first for you, another in the future" (6.19–21). The longer hymns differ from the shorter ones only because they develop the initial list of the god's attributes into a story, which elaborates on those attributes by explaining their origins. Thus, the long narrative of the *Hymn to Demeter* (2) flows from the initial identification of the goddess: "Here I sing fearsome, lovely-haired Demeter / And her trim-ankled child seized by Aidoneus" (2.1–2).

The many close connections between the *Hymns* and the Homeric epics does not mean, however, that the *Hymns'* author was Homer, as many in antiquity claimed, starting with the poet of the *Hymn to Apollo* (3), when he identifies himself as "A blind man" who "lives in rugged Chios" (3.172). For one thing, certain features of the *Hymns'* language indicate that they may be later in date than the Homeric epics, somewhat after 700 BCE, rather than somewhat before. Nor do all the *Hymns* in the collection necessarily belong to the same date; the collection, which comes to us through medieval manuscripts, may have been compiled many centuries after the earliest poems in it were composed, possibly in the third century BCE. Some, like the *Hymn to Ares* (8) and the *Hymn to Pan* (19), may be considerably later than most of the others. Finally, identifying Homer as the author of these *Hymns* would tell us very little anyway, since we have no real information about Homer and are not even sure that there was a single author of the two epics credited to him, the *Iliad* and the *Odyssey.*

Like the Delian festival that suggests a context for their performance, the *Homeric Hymns* were designed to bring together Greeks from many communities that were politically distinct. The Ionians included only those Greeks from Athens, the Aegean islands, and the central coast of present-day Turkey, but

the *Hymns* and some of the other religious institutions they cele-
brate were "Panhellenic," or open to all Greeks and designed to
unite all Greeks through their shared poetic and religious tradi-
tions. The gods of the Greek pantheon had local forms of wor-
ship that varied from city to city and were supported by myths
that linked a god to a particular place. The *Hymns* avoid those
local variants, associating the gods with broad Panhellenic cult
centers, like Delphi and Eleusis, that were visited by worshipers
from all over the Greek world. In the second part of the *Hymn to
Apollo* (3), the poet wonders which of the many stories about
Apollo to tell: "How will I find the right song, in so many?"
(3.207). Skipping over Apollo's many love affairs, which tend to
lead to the births of local heroes, he settles on the foundation of
the oracle. The gods of the *Hymns* are located nowhere in partic-
ular, or everywhere, which is one reason why these narratives
often include long geographical catalogs. Listing all the places
Leto visits in her frantic quest for a place to give birth, or all the
towns passed by Cretan sailors enlisted by Apollo as his priests,
the poet can link the god to many places at once. Through their
broad geographical reach, as well as through their focus on
defining moments of cosmic history, the *Hymns* speak to a wide
audience and make their appeal to the gods on behalf of all the
earthbound mortals who are subject to the rule of Zeus, all who
endure the gods' bitter gifts and enjoy their rich blessings.

Sheila Murnaghan
University of Pennsylvania

Note on the Text

The Greek text on which the translation is based is *The Homeric Hymns*, second edition, edited by T. W. Allen, W. R. Halliday, and E. E. Sikes (Oxford: Clarendon Press, 1936). The line numbers in the margins of the translation correspond to those of the Greek text, although the content of every line does not of course correspond exactly. Ellipses in the translation denote breaks in the text.

1

To Dionysus [Fragments]

Some say that you were born, O stitched-in god,
At windy Icarus or Dracanum
Or Naxos or Alpheus, the deep-whirled river,
To Semele and Zeus who loves the thunder.
Others, lord, claim that Thebes was your beginning—   5
Lies. Far from humankind, creation's father
Gave life to you unknown to white-armed Hera.
There is a forest-blossoming high peak, Nysa,
In far Phoenicia, near the streams of Egypt. . . .
"Will set up many gifts for her in temples. . . .   10
Mortals will bring you, every second year,
The gift of a full ritual hundred cattle."
The Cronian master lowered his black eyebrows.
The hair on his divine, immortal head
Fell forward and set high Olympus spinning.   15
So Zeus the counselor nodded and commanded.
Be kind, sewn god, woman-deranger. Singers
Chant you at the beginning and the ending.
No holy song is called to mind without you.

1: stitched-in god] Dionysus, god of wine and madness, son of Zeus and a
mortal woman Semele. Semele burned to death when, at her insistence,
Zeus visited her in his true form, the thunderbolt. Zeus took the unborn
Dionysus and sewed him into his own thigh until Dionysus was ready to be
born.

7: Hera] Zeus's jealous wife.

9–10: Egypt . . .] Here there seems to be a break between two sections of
what was once a much longer poem.

13: The Cronian master] Zeus, son of Cronus.

20 Joy to you, therefore, seam-born Dionysus—
And to Semele your mother, called Thyone.

2

To Demeter

Here I sing fearsome, lovely-haired Demeter
And her trim-ankled child seized by Aidoneus.
Far-seeing, thundering Zeus had sanctioned it.
Gold-sword, bright-grain Demeter did not know.
The girl played with the Sea's deep-bosomed daughters   5
In a lush field, picking hyacinths, bright violets,
Irises, crocuses, roses—and the narcissus,
Which the earth grew to trap the flower-faced girl,
By Zeus's tactics, for the host of many.
Gods whose life never ends and mortal people   10
Were dazzled by the flower when they saw it.
From a single root a hundred blossoms flourished
And smelled so sweet the whole wide sky above it
Laughed, and the whole earth and the salt sea laughed.
Enthralled, the girl stretched both hands toward the fine toy—   15
But the plain of Nysa, with its wide roads, opened:
And the lord Cronian, famous host of many,
Drove his immortal, leaping horses at her.
She was unwilling, caught in the gold chariot
That took her wailing, shrieking for the help of   20
Her father, son of Cronus, highest and greatest.
Yet no undying god or mortal heard her—

2: *trim-ankled child*] Persephone.
2: *Aidoneus*] God of the underworld, also known as Hades, brother of
Zeus.
9: *host of many*] Hades.
17: *Cronian*] Here Hades, like Zeus, the son of Cronus.

Not even the olive trees (with rich fruit) noticed.
Only bright-veiled and tender-hearted Hecate,
25 The daughter of Persaeus, in her grotto,
And the lord Sun, Hyperion's shining offspring,
Heard the girl call her father, son of Cronus—
But he sat far off in a prayer-filled shrine
And took fine gifts from mortals. By his offer
30 The host and the commander of so many,
The fame-rich son of Cronus, took his own niece
Away by force—his deathless horses drew them.
While still in sight of earth and starry heaven,
The sea's great currents and its clouds of fishes
35 And the sun's radiance, she still hoped to see
The tribes of gods again, and her dear mother,
And this hope soothed her brave mind in its anguish.
The mountain peaks, the sea depths gave an echo
Of her holy voice. Her queenly mother heard it.
40 Sharp was the pain that clutched her heart. Her own hands
Tattered the veil on her immortal hair.
She threw a dark-blue cloak around her shoulders
And darted birdlike, searching land and ocean.
Of all enduring gods and perishing people,
45 Nobody wished to tell the truth to her,
And birds that carry omens brought no message.
Nine days across the earth majestic Deo
Roamed, holding in her hands two flaming torches,
So anguished that she would not eat ambrosia,
50 Drink delicious nectar, or wash her body.
But when the tenth dawn came and brought its splendor,
Then, torch in hand, Hecate came to meet her,
And the words she spoke to her were full of news.

24: Hecate] A helpful, mediating goddess, later associated with witchcraft.
47: Deo] Another name for Demeter.

"Demeter, queen of seasons and their treasures,
What god above or mortal stole Persephone   55
And filled your heart with grief? Her voice alone
Reached me—I could not see who caused her shouting.
So much I know—so little, but told truly."
These were Hecate's words. She had no answer
From bright-haired Rhea's child—who dashed with her,   60
Torch in each hand, to Helios, the lookout
For gods and men, and stood before his horses.
The brightest of the goddesses harangued him.
"Helios, gods owe honor to each other.
Repay all I have said or done that pleased you.   65
I had a child, a beautiful, sweet blossom.
Across the sterile air I heard her shrieking,
As if from violence, but my eyes saw nothing.
But *your* rays from the glittering height of ether
Reach anywhere the land and sea themselves reach.   70
Say where my child is, tell me if you saw her.
Which of the gods or which of human mortals
Took her against her will, without my knowledge?"
Hyperion's offspring gave to her this answer:
"Lady Demeter, bright-haired Rhea's daughter,   .   75
I'll tell you, from respect and sympathy—
How you must miss your slender-ankled child!
No god but Zeus, cloud-gatherer, is guilty.
He made her over to his brother Hades
As his fine wife. To misty dark he took her   80
In a chariot, even though she shrieked in protest.
Goddess, you must give up your noisy grieving—
You'll have no benefit from endless anger.
Hades your own blood brother won't disgrace you
As son-in-law, for that wide-ruler's privilege   85

60: Rhea] Wife of Cronus, mother of Demeter.

Was from the start a third of all creation.
He is allotted kingship in his country."
He spoke these words, then shouted to his horses.
Like long-winged birds they sprang, with the quick chariot.
90 A grief more terrible and savage seized her.
Now angry with the dark-cloud son of Cronus,
She left the gathered gods on high Olympus
And went to humans' cities and their rich fields.
For a long time she covered up her beauty.
95 Men and loose-belted women did not know her
To look at, till she reached the house of Celeus,
Insightful ruler of perfumed Eleusis.
Grief in her heart, she sat down by the road,
By the Maiden's Well, where citizens drew water,
100 In the shadow that a bushy olive gave her;
Looking quite old, and long cut off from childbirth
And the gifts of garland-loving Aphrodite;
Like nurses of law-serving rulers' infants,
And storeroom keepers in their echoing mansions.
105 The daughters of Celeus, son of Eleusis,
There to draw water easily and take it
In bronze jugs to the house of their dear father,
Saw her—four girls like goddesses in fresh youth,
Callidice, Cleisidice, charming Demo,
110 Callithoë the eldest. They did not see
A god there: that is difficult for mortals.
But the girls spoke winged words as they stood near her.
"Where do you come from, Granny, and what kind of
Old person are you? You avoid the city?

86: third of all creation] When Zeus and his brothers divided up the universe, Zeus got the heavens, Poseidon the sea, and Hades the underworld. Zeus's gift of Persephone to Hades is a further step in this division.
102: Aphrodite] Goddess of love.

The halls are shady there and full of women. 115
Some are around your age and others younger;
All have kind words and treatment ready for you."
This the girls said. And the divine queen answered:
"Bless you, dear children—strangers of my own sex.
Here is my story. It is not improper 120
To tell you everything, because you ask me.
Doso is what my lady mother called me.
On the wide back of the sea I came, unwilling,
From Crete—the violence of some pirates brought me.
At Thoricus they landed with their swift ship. 125
We women crowded out, onto the shore
With our captors, and they set about with supper
Beside the stern, and yet my heart desired
No meal to make it glad. With stealth I hurried
Through the dark land away from arrogant masters. 130
I would not let them take me, a free woman,
Across the sea and turn me into trade goods.
This far my wandering leads but has not taught me
What country this might be, and of what people.
May all who have their mansions on Olympus 135
Supply you husbands, so that you have children,
Just as your parents wish. But you take pity. . . .
Dear children, kindly say which house to go to,
And for which man or woman I should labor
Gladly at tasks that suit an older woman. 140
Tenderly I could nurse a newborn baby
Held in my arms, care for the house, or make up
The lord's bed in the niche of a fine bedroom,
Or teach the household chores to younger women."
The virgin Callidice gave this answer 145

137: One or more lines appear to be missing from the manuscript in which
this poem is preserved.

(Of all the girls, she was the prettiest):
"Mother, the gods' gifts, even painful ones,
We mortals must accept. Gods are much stronger.
But I will give you clear directions, naming
150 All those who lead the people with their power
And their prestige, guarding the city's crown
Of towers with their advice and their just judgments:
Subtle-minded Triptolemus, Dioclus,
Polyxeinus, irreproachable Eumolpus,
155 Dolichus, and our own high-hearted father.
All of these men have wives to keep their mansions.
And not a single lady, once she saw you,
Would sneer at you and turn you from her doorstep.
They'll take you in, since you are like a goddess.
160 But if you like, wait—we will go back quickly
To our father's house and tell what you have told us
To our long-belted mother Metaneira.
She may not let another family get you!
The son she prayed for many years to have
165 Is growing up now in the well-built hall.
If you can raise him into full young manhood,
Then any women anywhere who see you
Will envy the rewards you have for it."
The goddess gave a nod. The girls filled up
170 Their bright jugs and returned with speed, exulting,
To their father's palace, where they told their mother
All they had seen and heard. She, in a flurry,
Sent them to offer wages to the woman,
As large as she might wish. As browse-contented
175 Heifers and does go prancing through spring pastures,
The girls ran down the sheltered path. They held up
The folds of their fine dresses; at their shoulders
Their hair was quivering like crocus petals.
Beside the road they found the glorious goddess,

Where they had left her. To their father's mansion 180
They took her. The divine one walked behind them,
Sorrowing in her heart, her head veiled, dark robe
Eddying around her slender, sacred feet.
They came soon to the mansion of Celeus—
Whom gods had raised—and entered. By a pillar, 185
Prop of the strong roof, sat their lady mother,
And on her lap her tender child was lying.
The girls ran up. Now *she* stood on the threshold,
Head at the ceiling, aura in the doorway.
Then pale fear, reverence, wonder seized the lady. 190
She stood and urged the other to be seated.
Demeter, bringer of seasons, giver of bright gifts,
Declined to touch the couch in all its splendor,
But stood there stubborn, lovely eyes averted.
Then shrewd Iambe set a well-built stool out, 195
And on it draped a fleece the shade of silver.
Sitting on this, Demeter pulled her veil
Over her face and sat in quiet sorrow—
Showing no warmth in either word or movement—
Unsmiling, eating nothing, drinking nothing— 200
Just pining for her daughter with the long belt.
But sharp Iambe with her many jokes
And sidelong wisecracks coaxed the heavenly queen
To smile and laugh and let her heart grow softer.
In later times as well she soothed the goddess. 205
Then Metaneira filled a cup with sweet wine
To give her. She replied she must not swallow

194: eyes averted] Demeter's withdrawn state, along with other details, such as the fleece she sits on and the special drink she asks for, gives a mythological origin for the ritual practices of the Eleusinian Mysteries.

195: Iambe] Iambe's name connects her to the iambic meter, used for poetry in honor of Demeter, and also for bawdy invective, originally in ritual contexts.

The deep red drink. She told her to mix water
With barley and soft pennyroyal for drinking.
210   The lady gave her this, as she was ordered,
And the majestic Deo drank, in ritual.
Then Metaneira of the fine belt spoke first:
"Welcome, my lady—for I think your parents
Were noble—in your eyes is a devout grace,
215   As in the eyes of kings, keepers of custom.
The bitter gifts of gods are ours to suffer.
Their yoke lies on our necks. Since you have come here,
Whatever I myself have, you may have it.
Bring up my late-born son, whom I'd lost hope for,
220   God-given prize for many years of praying.
If with your help he reaches full young manhood,
I'll give you such rewards that any woman
Who sees them will be overcome with envy."
Then lovely-garlanded Demeter answered,
225   "Great joy and blessings in return, my lady.
Gladly I'll take and raise him, as you urge me.
I doubt that witchcraft or the Undercutter
Will do him damage through his nurse's laxness.
I know a charm the Woodcutter will fall to.
230   I know a barrier to hateful sorcery."
She spoke, and with divine hands took the child
To her fragrant lap—much to his mother's pleasure.
Demophoön, bright son of Metaneira
Of the fine belt and the wise Celeus,
235   She nurtured in the palace. He grew, godlike;
He took no food or mother's milk. . . . Demeter
Breathed sweetly on him, cuddled him, and rubbed him
With ambrosia, just as if he were a god's child.
At night she hid him loglike in the strong fire.

227: Undercutter] This and "Woodcutter" in line 229 refer to those who
practice magic by harvesting and using efficacious plants.

His parents did not know. They only marveled   240
How speedily he grew—and with divine looks.
His death and old age would have been prevented,
But ignorant, fine-belted Metaneira,
Who played the night spy from her fragrant bedroom,
Saw it. Striking her thighs, she gave a shrill cry,   245
Beside herself with terror for her infant
These were the wailing, winged words that she spoke:
"Demophoön, my child, the stranger buries
You deep in flame—for me a crushing torment."
The shining goddess heard her speak in anguish.   250
Bright-crowned Demeter then was filled with frenzy:
With her immortal hands she took the dear child
(Born beyond hope in the palace) from the fire
And threw him to the floor in terrible anger
And spoke to Metaneira of the fine belt: 255
"Idiot mortals, who cannot foresee
Your fate—a good or bad one coming toward you.
You cannot mend the mindless thing you did.
Implacable Styx, water the gods swear by,
Be witness, I was going to spare him old age   260
And death, and give him endless honor also.
He cannot now escape the fiends of death—
But since I held him sleeping on my lap,
He will possess lifelong, unwithering honor.
Once he has grown up through the circling years,   265
Eternally the Eleusinians' children
Will struggle with each other in fierce battle.
I am revered Demeter. From me is given
The greatest help and joy to gods and mortals.
Let all the people build me a great temple   270
Shading an altar, by the city's steep wall,

267: fierce battle] Ritual war games, through which Demophoön will be
perennially honored.

Above Callichorus, on the jutting hilltop.
There I will teach my mysteries; from now on
The holy ritual will soothe my spirit."
275 The goddess said no more, but grew and altered.
She shed old age, and beauty breathed around her.
The clothes she wore gave off a lovely fragrance.
From her immortal body light beamed. Bright hair
Streamed on her shoulders. Like a flash of lightning,
280 An incandescence filled the well-built mansion.
She left the hall. The lady's knees subsided
That moment—she was speechless—she forgot
To take her darling son up from the floor.
His sisters heard his pitiful cries and dashed
285 From their rich-covered couches. One among them
Cuddled him in her arms against her bosom.
One lit the fire. Another rushed with soft feet
To her mother's fragrant room to lift her up.
Gathered around the gasping child, they bathed him
290 And fondled him, but still his heart was hardened
And disappointed in his present tending.
All night they shook with fear, propitiating
The glorious goddess, but when dawn appeared,
Celeus the ruler heard the whole true story,
295 As lovely-garlanded Demeter ordered,
And he assembled all his countless people
And made them build an altar and rich shrine
On the high ground for shining-haired Demeter.
They listened, and obeyed his proclamation:
300 The walls rose as the goddess had commanded.
When they were done, withdrawing from their labor,
Each one went home. But yellow-haired Demeter
Sat there alone, far from the blissful gods,
Sick with the absence of her loose-sashed daughter.
305 Then for a year she made the generous land

Merciless, grim for mortals. The earth let rise
No seed, since glorious-crowned Demeter hid it.
For nothing oxen drew their squads of curved plows.
White barley seed fell thickly without profit.
Her ruthless famine would have made away   310
With humankind, and all the splendid things
It gives and sacrifices to Olympus
Had Zeus not taken notice and considered.
He first sent gold-winged Iris down to summon
Demeter of the lovely form, the bright hair.   315
He spoke, and she obeyed Zeus of the dark clouds,
The son of Cronus: quick feet brought her earthward,
To the fortress of Eleusis rich in fragrance,
And there she found Demeter in her dark cloak,
And from her mouth this greeting fluttered outward.   320
"Demeter, Zeus whose wisdom has no ending
Summons you to the clans of the undying.
Do not keep Zeus's word from its fulfillment."
This supplicating speech did not convince her.
The father then dispatched each of the blessèd,   325
Who live forever: one by one arriving,
They urged her, and the bribes they named were many:
Glorious objects and her choice of honors.
No one subdued her spirit and convinced her.
Her stubborn rage rejected all their speeches.   330
She would not climb Olympus in its fragrance,
She said, or let the land send up a harvest,
Before her own eyes saw her sweet-faced daughter.
Loud-thundering, wide-seeing Zeus, who heard this,
Sent down to Erebus the Argus-killer   335

314: Iris] Messenger of the gods.
335: to Erebus the Argus-killer] Erebus is the gloom of the underworld; the Argus-killer is Hermes, a god who is often Zeus's envoy.

With his gold wand, to try sweet words with Hades,
Win pure Persephone from misty darkness,
And lead her to the light where other gods are,
To her mother's sight, and end her mother's anger.
340 Obedient Hermes, starting from Olympus,
Plummeted to the earth's invisible places,
And there he found lord Hades in his palace,
His timid consort on the couch beside him—
Unwilling, longing for her far-off mother,
345 Who schemed revenge against the blissful gods.
The forceful Argus-killer stood before them:
"Dusky-haired Hades, king of all the perished,
Father Zeus ordered me to bring Persephone
The noble out of Erebus to join us,
350 Since at the sight of her, her mother's fury
Against the gods will fade. She now plans outrage,
The end of the weak tribes of earthly mortals:
She hides the seed below the earth, destroying
Our tribute. In her great rage, she rejects us
355 And sits apart in her sweet-smelling temple,
Up in the craggy fortress of Eleusis."
He said this. Aidoneus, king of the dead,
Grimaced, obeying Zeus the ruler's orders.
Quickly he told Persephone the prudent,
360 "Persephone, go to your dark-robed mother,
And foster in your heart a gentle temper—
And do not let what happened make you wretched.
Among the gods I'll be a fitting husband,
As father Zeus's brother. While you live here,
365 All things that live and move will be in your charge,
And yours will be the greatest holy honors.
The sinners who do not appease your power,
Offering proper gifts and sacrifices
In pure rites, will for all time feel your vengeance."

Now wise Persephone heard and was elated. 370
She eagerly got up. But canny Hades
First slipped her a sweet pomegranate kernel
To eat: he made provision that the modest,
Dark-robed Demeter could not keep her daughter.
Then Aidoneus, lord of many, yoked 375
His deathless horses to the golden chariot,
And she got in, and the strong Argus-killer
Beside her gripped the reins and whip and hurried
Out of the palace. Readily the horses
Took flight and swiftly finished their long journey. 380
No rivers, nor the sea, nor grassy valleys,
Nor mountain peaks could block the heavenly horses.
They rushed on through the endless air above these,
To where Demeter, bright-crowned goddess, waited
Before her scented shrine. She saw and bolted 385
Like a maenad down a forest-shaded mountain.
And for her part, Persephone left the horses
And chariot when she saw her mother's fine eyes—
Leaped down and ran and threw her arms around her.
Even before she let her darling child go, 390
Demeter grew suspicious. With a grim fear,
She halted her caresses and addressed her:
"Surely you ate no food in that deep place,
My child? Tell—do not hide it. We must both know.
Can you return to me from hateful Hades, 395
And to the brooding-clouded son of Cronus,
To stay with us, adored by all immortals?
Or must you go back to earth's secret places
To live a third of every set of seasons—
The rest with me, though, and the other deities? 400
When the earth blooms with lovely-scented flowers

386: maenad] An ecstatic female worshiper of Dionysus.

Of every kind, then from the haze and darkness
You will come up, and gods and men will marvel.
But how did the strong host of many trick you?"
405 Persephone the beautiful answered her:
"Dear mother, I'll tell everything that happened.
When the Argus-killer came, kind messenger
From my Cronian father and the others living
In heaven, to bring me up from Erebus,
410 So at the sight of me your terrible anger
Against the gods would end—with joy I jumped up.
But in my mouth he put some pomegranate,
Sweet food—by force, against my will, I ate it.
How through the cunning of my Cronian father
415 He took me to the earth's invisible places—
I'll tell you everything, just as you ask me.
All of us roamed around the lovely meadow,
Leucippe, Phaeno, Ianthe, Electra,
Callirhoë, Melita, Iache, Rhodea,
420 Tyche, Melobosis, flower-faced Ocyrhoë,
Chryseïs, Ianeira, and Acaste;
Admete, Rhodope, Pluto, sweet Calypso,
Styx, Urania, charming Galaxaura,
Strife-waking Pallas, arrow-pouring Artemis.
425 We had our fun there picking pretty flowers:
Soft crocus mixed with hyacinth and iris—
Rosebud and lily—wonders—and the narcissus,
Which the broad earth sent growing like a crocus.
I picked it in delight. The earth beneath it
430 Gaped, and the strong lord, host of all the perished,
Took me below the ground in his gold chariot—
But I resisted, and I shrieked in protest.

424: Artemis] Along with the nymphs already named, Persephone's play-
mates include two virgin Olympian goddesses: Pallas Athena and Artemis.

Though what I tell is painful, it is truthful."
All of that day they spent in perfect concord.
Great was the joy they lent each other's spirit,   435
Closely embracing, free from all their sorrow,
Exchanging rapture. Bright-veiled Hecate
Came near. Time after time she clutched the child
Of pure Demeter; and in after-ages
The goddess was her servant and companion.   440
Deep-thundering, wide-seeing Zeus sent word now
Through bright-haired Rhea to dark-cloaked Demeter
To join the gods' clans, choosing any honors—
He promised this—among the deathless beings.
And he consented that, as the year circled,   445
The girl would spend a third in misty darkness,
And two thirds with her mother and the other
Immortals. The goddess did not disobey.
She rushed down from the summit of Olympus
To the fertile richness of the Rharian plain—   450
The richness that had been: the land was useless,
All leafless. Demeter of the pretty ankles
Hid the white barley cunningly. But later,
As springtime flourished, grain would stream in long ears,
And these would soon fill up the fertile furrows   455
When the time came for tying into sheaves.
There she alighted from the barren ether.
The two were overjoyed to see each other.
Shining-veiled Rhea then addressed Demeter:
"Come, child: far-seeing and loud-thundering Zeus   460
Summons you to the nations of immortals
For any holy privileges you choose.
He sanctions that your child will stay a third part
Of the circling year beneath the misty darkness,
But live with you and all of us for two thirds.   465
He gives his nod for this to be accomplished.

Listen, my child: give up your stubborn fury
Toward the son of Cronus hiding in a dark cloud,
And quickly give mankind their nurturing harvest."
470 She spoke. Sweet-garlanded Demeter listened,
And hurried crops to daylight through the rich loam.
The whole wide earth was heaped with leaves and flowers.
She went then to the kings, keepers of custom,
Triptolemus, Diocles driver of horses,
475 Strong Eumolpus, Celeus the commander,
And taught all these her proper rites and mysteries—
478 Sacred, inviolable, not to be questioned
Or told of. Fear of the gods holds back the voice.
480 Yet any earthly man is blessed who sees them.
The uninitiated have no portion
Like his, when dead, below in mist and darkness.
The shining deity gave these instructions.
Now the two joined the others on Olympus.
485 Alongside thunder-loving Zeus they live there,
Revered and holy. Happy among the earthbound
Is anyone who feels their love and kindness.
They quickly send a guest into his great house:
Wealth, who gives all good things to mortal people.
490 Come, you who keep Eleusis with its sweet scents,
Current-encircled Paros and rocky Antron:
Queen Deo, ruler of shining gifts and seasons—
Persephone as well, your lovely daughter—
Please bless your singer with a cheerful living.
495 I pledge your story, then a new recital.

3

To Apollo

To Delian Apollo

Apollo the far-shooter I'll fix in mind.
All gods but one rise quickly from their seats,
All but one shake while he is striding toward them
Through Zeus's house, drawing his glittering bow.
Leto remains by Zeus who loves the thunder.   5
She first unstrings the bow and shuts the quiver,
Then takes the weapon off his burly shoulders
And hangs it from a gold peg, on a pillar
Of his father's hall, and leads him to his throne.
His father hands him nectar in a gold cup,   10
Greeting his cherished son. The gods around them
Can now sit down. And joy fills lady Leto
At the great power of her bowman offspring.
Hail, blessèd Leto with your shining children:
Lordly Apollo, Artemis arrow-pourer.   15
One in Ortygia, one in rocky Delos
Was born (you leaned on the long Cynthian ridge,
Beside the palm tree and Inopus waters).
How can I make one song from all your glory?
Yours is the grassy reach of singing, Phoebus,   20
Across the fertile mainland and the islands.
You love the lookouts and the towering headlands
Of the steep mountains, and the seaward rivers,
The beaches leaning toward the sea, the harbors.

5: *Leto*] Apollo's parents are Zeus and Leto.
20: *Phoebus*] "Shining," one of Apollo's most common epithets.

19

25 Should I tell how you, the world's joy, came from Leto,
    Who leaned on Cynthus on the rocky island,
    Delos in flowing seas? On both sides black waves
    Rushed toward the dry land under shrill winds' power.
    So you were born to be the lord of mortals.
30 Through Crete and to the polity of Athens,
    Euboea known for ships, Aegine island,
    Aegae, Eiresiae, sea-perched Peparethus,
    Thracian Athos, Pelion's giant upreach,
    Samos near Thrace, the shadowy hills of Ida,
35 Autocane's sharp height, Scyros, Phocaea,
    Sturdy-built Imbros, mist-encircled Lemnos,
    Aeolus's son Macar's holy Lesbos,
    Chios the richest island in the water,
    Craggy Mimas, Corycus's high summits,
40 Radiant Claros, Aesagea's dagger mountain,
    Moist Samos and the sharp crags of Mycale,
    Miletus, Cos, and the Meropian city,
    Sheer Cnidos, and the hard winds of Carpathos,
    Naxos, Paros too, and stony Rhenaea—
45 To these, in labor with the archer, Leto
    Traveled to find a homeland for her child.
    But every country shook with fear, none daring,
    Even the wealthiest, to welcome Phoebus.
    But then the lady Leto came to Delos
50 And sent out fluttering words in an inquiry:
    "Delos, if you allow Phoebus Apollo,
    My son, to make his temple and his home here—
    Because, you know, no other god will take you—
    Never will you have wealth in sheep or cattle
55 Or grain, or any green thing in abundance;
    But with Apollo the far-worker's temple,

45: the archer] Apollo.

All humankind will gather here and bring you
Hundred-strong herds. Wonderfully rich, the savor
Of burning fat will rise. Those living in you
Will eat the gifts of strangers, not your thin yields." 60
She spoke, and Delos made a happy answer:
"Leto, excellent daughter of great Coeus,
I'd welcome the lord archer being born here.
It's true, I have a deadly reputation,
And here's a way to get tremendous honor— 65
But Leto, what I fear should not be hidden:
They say Apollo in his arrogance
Will lord it over everyone—immortals,
And mortal men as well on fields where wheat grows.
My heart and mind are full of sickening fear 70
That when he sees the sunlight for the first time,
He'll feel contempt for me, a stony island,
And kick me over into the broad ocean.
While a great downsurge sweeps above my head
Forever, he will choose another country 75
And build his shrine and plant his shadowy forests—
Black seals and many-footed things will settle
In me, untroubled, where there are no people.
But goddess, if you dare to swear a great oath
That here he first will build a splendid temple, 80
An oracle for mortals, he can go then
To all the world in his great fame and glory."
She spoke. And Leto swore a great, divine oath:
"Be witness, Earth, and the wide Sky above me,
And the slow Stygian stream (this is the pledge 85
The blessèd gods hold greatest and most fearful):
Here the god's fragrant altar and his precinct
Will always be—and you will be his favorite."
And when the oath she offered was completed,
The lord far-shooter's birth made Delos joyful. 90

But unexpected pains, nine days and nine nights,
Pierced Leto. Yet the goddesses around her
Were all the noblest: Rhea and Dione,
Ichnaea, Themis, sighing Amphitrite—
95 Immortal ladies—all but white-armed Hera,
Who waited in cloud-gathering Zeus's palace,
And birth-pain Eileithyia, who did not know.
She sat on high Olympus under gold clouds,
Since white-armed Hera's jealousy and cunning
100 Kept her away while Leto of the bright hair
Was laboring with a strong and perfect male child.
Dispatching Iris from the settled island,
They sent for Eileithyia with a promise
Of a huge, nine-cubit necklace made of gold threads:
105 Iris must call her out past white-armed Hera,
Whose words would turn her back from her commission.
And when the swift, wind-footed Iris heard this,
She ran and soon made nothing of the distance.
And when she reached the gods' home, steep Olympus,
110 Quickly she called and summoned Eileithyia
Out of her palace with a swarm of fine words—
Exactly as the goddesses had ordered—
And coaxed the heart inside her to the purpose.
They went ahead, like shy doves in their movements.
115 When birth-pain Eileithyia came to Delos,
Then only did birth's urgency seize Leto.
She grasped a palm tree in her arms, knees driven
Into the soft grass. Earth, beneath her, smiled.
The god leaped lightward; every goddess shouted.
120 Then, Phoebus of the holy shriek, they washed you

95: Hera] Zeus's jealous wife.
97: Eileithyia] Goddess of childbirth, who helps women in labor.
102: Iris] Messenger of the gods.

Reverently in pure water and swaddled you
In a soft new cloth and wrapped gold bands around you.
Apollo of the gold sword never nursed.
Themis instead gave nectar and ambrosia,
Sweet offerings from holy hands, and Leto   125
Rejoiced to be the forceful archer's mother.
But Phoebus, when the holy food was in you,
The gold bands would not hold you as you struggled—
Nothing could bind you—knotted ropes came loose.
Apollo spoke among the deathless women: 130
"I will be patron of the lyre and curved bow,
And prophet of the changeless will of Zeus."
Now long-haired Phoebus, god who shoots from far off,
Went walking on the land with its wide highways.
The goddesses were all astonished. Delos   135
Was heaped with gold by Zeus and Leto's son.
Elated that the god had made his home there
Among all lands and islands, as the dearest,
She blossomed like a forest-covered hilltop.
You, the lord archer, silver-bowed Apollo,   140
Sometimes go striding over rugged Cynthus,
Or wander through the islands full of people.
You claim a crowd of temples, throngs of copses.
You love the lookout places and the headlands
Of soaring mountains, ocean-chasing rivers—   145
And yet you have your greatest joy in Delos.
To worship you, the trailing-robed Ionians
Gather there—men, their shy wives, and their children.
There boxing, dancing, and the work of singers

124: Themis] Goddess associated with order and justice.

147: Ionians] A subgroup of the Greeks living in Athens, the Aegean
islands, and the central coast of present-day Turkey. Their main cult center
was on Delos, where they held an annual festival for Apollo.

150   Commemorates you in diverting contests.
      Whoever sees this people all together
      Would say that they were ageless and immortal.
      Their grace would hold his eyes, his heart would relish
      The sight of men and suavely belted women,
155   And the wealth brought with them in their speedy ships.
      There is one more imperishable wonder:
      The Delian entourage of the far-striker,
      The girls who sing, to start, about Apollo,
      Next Leto and her arrow-pouring daughter;
160   They call to mind then all the men and women
      Of the time gone, to charm the gathered nations.
      They mimic every sort of voice and music;
      People, if they could hear, would think the singing
      Came from themselves—it is so full of truth.
165   Come now with Artemis, bless us, Apollo.
      Singers, goodbye, but keep the memory of me;
      And when, out of earth's people, there arrives here
      A foreigner with hard-earned knowledge, asking
      Whom you young girls like best among the singers
170   Who visit, whom you find most entertaining,
      All of you give this man a single answer:
      "A blind man, and he lives in rugged Chios:
      All of his songs will be the best forever."
      And I in turn will carry your fame with me
175   To every well-built city where I wander.
      The hearers will believe the truth I tell them.
      I'll never stop my praise of the far-shooter,
      Silver-bowed son of Leto of the bright hair.

159: arrow-pouring daughter] Apollo's sister Artemis.
172: Chios] By describing himself this way, the singer claims to be Homer.

To Pythian Apollo*

Charming Maeonia is your domain, lord,
And Lycia, and Miletus, sweet sea city;   180
You rule in person over sea-washed Delos.
The son of marvelous Leto makes his journey,
Playing a hollow lyre, toward stony Pytho,
Wearing divine, sweet-smelling clothes. The strings sound
With ringing beauty under the gold plectrum.   185
From earth then to Olympus quick as thinking
He comes, to Zeus's house, where the gods gather,
And quickly draws them to his hymning lyre.
All of the Muses in their sweet responsion
Sing of the gods' eternal gifts, the hardships   190
Of humans at the hands of the immortals,
Our mindless, helpless lives that never find
A cure for death, a guard against old age.
The smooth-haired Graces and the cheerful Hours,
Zeus's child Aphrodite, Harmony,   195
And Youth dance there, hands on each other's wrists.
And Ares, and the sharp-eyed Argus-killer,
Perform with them; and Artemis, arrow-pourer,
Apollo's sister—hardly plain or stunted
But towering and a wonder in her beauty.   200

---

*To Pythian Apollo] At this point, the poem's subject changes from Apollo's
birth and worship on Delos to his foundation of the oracle at Delphi, in the
area known as Pytho. The two sections may have originally been separate
hymns.

189: the Muses] Nine goddesses, daughters of Zeus and Mnemosyne
("Memory"), who represent singing and dancing, and later become indi-
vidual patrons of the various arts and intellectual pursuits.

195: Aphrodite] Goddess of love.

197: Argus-killer] Ares is god of war; the Argus-killer is the divine messen-
ger and god of thieves and travelers, Hermes.

Phoebus Apollo dances to his lyre
With fine, high steps and brightness rayed around him.
His rapid feet and precious tunic glow.
And gold-haired Leto and the counselor Zeus
205   Are full of pleasure in their great hearts, seeing
Their dear son frisk among immortal gods.
How will I find the right song, in so many?
Shall it be about the lover's expeditions?
How once you went to court the child of Azan
210   With well-horsed, godlike Ischys, son of Elatius,
With Phorbas, child of Triops, with Ereutheus,
Or as Leucippus and his wife's companion. . . .
On foot, by chariot? Triops could not beat him.
Or how you, archer god, at the beginning,
215   Sought where to build an oracle for mortals?
You came down from Olympus to Pieria,
Then passed by sandy Lectus, Enienae,
The Perrhaebi—and you quickly reached Iolcus.
You walked Cenaeum, maritime Euboea.
220   On the Lelantine plain you stood, deciding
To make no temple and no tree-rich glade there.
But next, far-shooter, crossing the Euripus,
You climbed the green and holy hill, but left it
Quickly for Mycalessus and Teumessus,
225   Bedded in grass, and Thebes, covered in forests.
No one was living yet in holy Thebes.
In Thebes there were no paths, there were no highways
Over a wheat-spread plain, but only forest.
From there you traveled on, archer Apollo,
230   And reached Poseidon's shining grove, Onchestus.

212: Something is either missing or garbled at this point in the manuscripts
in which this poem is preserved.
230: Poseidon] God of the sea and of horses.

New-broken colts there pant relief from pulling
Their handsome vehicles, and skillful drivers
Jump to the ground and walk the road. Their horses
Rattle the empty and unguided chariots.
All that are broken in the tree-rich forest   235
Are overturned. The horses are looked after.
This is the primal ritual. The drivers
Pray to the priest. The chariots are the god's share.
From here, archer Apollo, you proceeded
And touched on Cephissus with its clear streams,   240
The dash of its sweet water from Lilaea.
You forded it, passed towered Ocalea,
Far-worker, and reached grassy Haliartus,
And now approached the peaceful place, Telphusa,
Where you chose to make your temple and thick groves.   245
You stood there on the spring's edge and addressed her:
"Telphusa, I propose to build a temple,
A splendid oracle, and men will come here
Driving their gifts, herds of whole ritual hundreds.
Inhabitants of the rich Peloponnesus   250
And Europe and the islands washed with currents
Will come with questions. I will give true counsel
To all, in prophecies in my rich temple."
Phoebus Apollo quickly laid foundations—
Very long, solid, wide. But when she saw them,   255
Telphusa made this speech, in her heart's anger:
"Phoebus, far-working lord, hear and consider:
You have in mind to build a lovely temple,
An oracle for mortals, who will always
Drive their herds here for you in perfect hundreds.   260

244: *Telphusa*] Both a spring near Delphi and the nymph associated with it.
251: *Europe*] The part of mainland Greece north of the Gulf of Corinth;
the Peloponnesus (line 250) is the large peninsula to the south.

But let me give you something to consider.
The stomp of speedy horses, and mules slurping
From my holy springs, will irk you constantly.
Everyone coming here will want to ogle
265 Fine chariots and hear the thud of horses,
In spite of your great temple and its treasures.
Listen—though you are dominant and better
Than me, lord, and your power is enormous.
Instead, build in the hollow of Parnassus,
270 At Crisa. No swank chariots, no fast horses
Will clatter there around the well-built altar.
Men's famous tribes, acclaiming you as Healer,
Will bring you gifts, and you will be delighted
At first-class sacrifices from your neighbors."
275 Her speech convinced Apollo and accomplished
That her name would be known there, not the archer's.
Onward you went, far-striking god Apollo,
And reached the city of the savage Phlegians.
Without a thought for Zeus these men inhabit
280 A lovely glen by the Cephisian lake.
From there you hurried toward the ridge at Crisa;
Parnassus, topped with snow, stood overhead.
A slope turns toward the west. A cliff above it
Hangs, and a rough and lonely glen runs under.
285 Phoebus the noble made a resolution
That a majestic temple would be built there:
"I mean to build a graceful temple here,
An oracle for humankind, who always
Will drive me gifts, herds of a hundred cattle.
290 Inhabitants of the rich Peloponnesus
And Europe and the islands ringed with currents
Will seek my oracle. I will give all these
True guidance for the future in my rich shrine."
Apollo spoke, and laid out the foundations,

Wide, solid, and very long. And a stone threshold   295
Was placed by the sons of Erginus, Trophonius,
And Agamedes, friends of the deathless gods.
The endless human nations raised a temple
Of carved stone, to be sung about forever.
A lovely spring flowed near. The noble son   300
Of Zeus killed a huge snake with his stout bow there,
A savage, bloated monster, who brought outrage
Continually against the country's people
And slender-footed sheep—a gory curse.
She took as foster child from gold-throned Hera   305
Fierce Typhaon, hateful hurt for mankind,
Born out of Hera's rage at Zeus the father,
When he gave birth to glorious Athena
From his own head. The lady Hera, furious,
Blurted in the assembly of immortals: 310
"All of you, gods and goddesses, take notice:
Cloud-gathering Zeus is first to mortify me.
I was the one he made his honored wife.
Without me, though, he had gray-eyed Athena,
Shining even among divine immortals.   315
But out of me the maimed child you can all see . . .
Hephaestus with his warped legs is what *I* have.
I grabbed him, slung him into the wide ocean.
But the silver-slippered child of Nereus, Thetis,
Took him and cared for him, she and her sisters—   320
I wish she'd done the gods another favor.
Ingenious felon, what will you contrive now?

301: snake] Named Pytho, as we learn later (line 372).
316: One or more lines appear to be missing from the manuscripts in which
this poem is preserved.
319: Thetis] A powerful sea-goddess, important in the Troy legend as the
mother of Achilles.

How *could* you give Athena life without me?
Could I not do it? I am called your consort
325 Among the deathless ones who own high heaven.
325a Think what I might concoct against you someday—
In fact, I'll engineer the birth of *my* child,
Superb among the death-forgetting deities.
I will not shame the holy bed we share—
But neither will I enter it. I'm staying
330 Away from you—but still among immortals."
After this speech the cow-eyed lady Hera
Departed in her rage and swiftly made
This prayer, slapping the ground to rouse its power:
"Earth, and broad Sky above us, listen to me!
335 And god- and man-engendering Titans living
Below, around the massive gulf of Tartarus:
All of you, hear. Give me a child apart
From Zeus, but just as strong—no, even stronger,
As Zeus was stronger than his father Cronus."
340 She spoke and smacked the surface with her strong hand.
The rich earth shuddered. When the goddess saw it,
The heart inside her reveled at fulfillment.
From that time on until a year was finished,
She shunned the bed of Zeus the perspicacious
345 And the elaborate throne where she had once sat
Constructing clever plans to tell her husband,
And stayed instead inside her prayer-filled temples
Relishing gifts—the soft-eyed lady Hera.
But when the days and months were all completed,
350 The year revolved, the seasons' ring perfected,

325a: This line has been added to the Greek text because it is evidently part
of the original poem.
335: Titans] The generation of gods before Zeus and the other Olympians,
including Zeus's parents Cronus and Rhea. After defeating them in battle,
Zeus imprisoned them in Tartarus, the deepest part of the underworld.

She gave birth. It was unlike gods or humans—
Typhaon, savage pestilence for mankind.
Cow-eyed queen Hera heaped bad things together:
Grabbed him and took him to the willing she-snake.
While *he* inflicted crimes on famous peoples,   355
Everyone *she* found met their swooping death-day—
Until the lord far-worker sent an arrow
To overpower her. Broken in her torment,
She gasped and rolled supine across the landscape.
A scream rose huge, prodigious. Through the forest   360
She writhed in ring on ring and spat her spirit
Out with her gore. At last Apollo boasted,
"Lie here and rot, on the man-nurturing ground.
You will not be a blight to living mortals.
Feeding on what the fertile land produces,   365
They'll bring here offerings of perfect hundreds.
Typhoeus and the infamous Chimaera
Cannot stop death that lays you on this hard bed.
Black earth and bright Hyperion will rot you."
He said this, gloating. Shadow veiled her eyes.   370
She festered there beneath the holy Sun's strength.
Pytho is named from this. They call Apollo
Pythian lord because in this spot rotted
The grisly creature in the stabbing Sun's glare.
And then at last Phoebus Apollo realized   375
How he'd been cheated by the lovely fountain.
He quickly reached Telphusa in his anger
And, standing very near, spoke to her these words:

357: far-worker] Apollo.

367: Chimaera] Typhoeus is another name for Typhaon; the Chimaera is his descendant, a fire-breathing monster with elements of snake, goat, and lion.

369: Hyperion] An epithet for Helios the Sun.

372: is named from this] The name of the snake and of the place she once ruled is here connected to a Greek verb, *puthô*, meaning "to rot."

"Telphusa, your deception had no chance
380 To keep this pretty spot for your sweet water.
My fame will live here too, and not yours only."
Apollo lord far-worker shouldered a bluff
Down in a stream of stone to hide her off-springs
And built an altar in the woody thicket
385 Next to the lovely spring. All those who pray there
Give him the name Telphusian, invoking
The god who shamed Telphusa's holy currents.
Phoebus Apollo wondered in his heart
Which men to muster to perform his mysteries,
390 To be his servants up in rugged Pytho.
And as he thought, the wine-dark seascape showed him
A fast ship, with a crew of many fine men,
Cretans out of Minoan Cnossos—that race
Who sacrifice to Phoebus of the gold sword,
395 And bring out the decrees of lord Apollo
From the bay tree in the hollow of Parnassus.
They sailed in their black ship to trade for profit
With the inhabitants of sandy Pylos.
Phoebus Apollo met them now, appearing
400 Out on the sea, dolphin-disguised, and hurtled
Onto their swift ship. Fearsome, huge he lay there.
No soul among the crew could recognize him.
He thrashed around and rattled the ship's timbers.
The men sat quiet on the ship in terror,
405 Not loosening the hollow black boat's tackle,
Not taking down the sail above the dark prow.
In the direction that the ox-thongs sent them

396: bay tree] The bay, or laurel, was sacred to Apollo; the priestess who
was the medium for Apollo's prophecies was said to use the leaves in various
ways, shaking them on the tree, burning them, and even chewing them
before giving her responses.

They skimmed. A rushing south wind urged their quick ship
Forward, and first they left behind Malea,
Then off Laconian land they reached Taenarum,   410
The sea-ringed town, district of mortal-charming
Helios. Always in that splendid country
The deep-fleeced sheep of the majestic Sun graze.
They longed to land, get off, and take account of
The marvel on the deck—and then to see   415
Whether the monster on the hollow ship's floor
Stayed or leaped over to the fish-filled salt swell.
The well-built ship would not obey the rudder,
But took a route by the Peloponnesus.
Apollo lord far-worker made the wind blow   420
And steered with ease. Accomplishing its journey,
The ship reached Arene, sweet Argyphea,
Thyron (the ford of Alpheus), fine Aepy,
And sandy Pylos (with its native people).
It passed by Cruni, Chalcis, and by Dyme,   425
By glittering Elis ruled by the Epei.
Glad with the wind from Zeus, it shot toward Pherae.
Above the clouds appeared the peak of Ithaca,
Dulichium, Same, Zachynthos forests.
Once they had circled the whole Peloponnesus,   430
There showed ahead the mammoth gulf at Crisa,
The rich peninsula cut off along it.
A clear west gale came down at Zeus's order,
Blustering from remote skies, and the ship fled,
Crossing with speed the ocean's bitter water.   435
They swept back then in sun and dawn's direction,
With lord Apollo, Zeus's son, their leader.
They sailed to far-seen Crisa, rich in vineyards.
On the harbor's sands the voyaging hull was grounded.

412: Helios] The Sun.

440   The lord far-worker soared up from the vessel,
Bright as a star, though it was noon. Around him
The sparks swarmed, and their brilliance reached the far sky.
He stepped into his shrine past precious tripods,
And there he kindled flame to show his arrows.
445   The brightness conquered Crisa, and a shout rose
From Crisan wives and pretty-belted daughters
At Phoebus in his onslaught—each felt terror.
From there, quick as a thought, he flew aboard ship,
An energetic, strong man in appearance,
450   A youth whose long hair fell around broad shoulders—
And let these words go flying out at them:
"Where do you come from on the roads of water,
Strangers? Who are you? Traders? Are you reckless
Pirates roaming around the sea and preying
455   On strangers at the risk of your own lives?
Why do you sit there baffled and unable
To disembark or stow the black ship's tackle?
Those traveling for their living have this privilege,
When their black ships exchange the sea for seaboard:
460   The sailors, with their bellies full of tiredness,
Are gripped with longing for—instead—some good food."
His words brought courage back into their hearts.
The Cretan leader spoke and made an answer:
"Stranger, since you are not like any mortal,
465   But like the deathless gods in height and beauty,
Have health and joy and all the gods can give you!
Tell me this truly, let me understand it:
What is this land, this town? Who are these people?
With other plans we crossed the sea's great chasm
470   From Crete to Pylos—we are all proud Cretans.

443: tripods] Three-legged cauldrons, often presented to the gods as
offerings.

Now in our boat we land here, quite unwilling,
Out of our way and longing for the way home.
One of the gods has brought us by compulsion."
Apollo the far-worker gave this answer:
"Strangers who lived near richly wooded Cnossos,   475
You forfeit the return you once expected
To your lovely town and prepossessing mansions,
And much-loved wives. Here you will keep my temple:
It will be rich, and great crowds will revere it.
I am the son of Zeus, the proud Apollo.   480
I brought you here across the sea's great chasm—
Not doing harm but making you the stewards
Of a rich shrine mankind will stand in awe of.
The gods' plans will be yours to know—by their will
Your honor will be endless and unbroken.   485
But come now and obey without delaying.
To start, untie the thongs and take the sails down,
Then heave the speedy ship up on the dry land,
Take out your goods and strip the straight ship's gear.
Where breakers reach the shore, construct an altar,   490
And light a fire and offer up white barley,
And pray together, standing round the altar.
Since at the very start, on murky ocean,
My dolphin form jumped into your fast vessel,
Pray to me as the Dolphin god. The altar   495
Will be the Dolphin's lookout through the ages.
Next, have your dinner by the rapid dark ship.
Pour wine out to the blessèd on Olympus.
But once you're rid of any lust for good food,
Come with me, chanting, 'Glory to the Healer!'   500
To the place where you will keep my wealthy temple."

495: *Dolphin god*] Apollo was worshiped as *Delphinius*, "Dolphin god,"
especially by sailors.

He spoke. They heard with reverence and obeyed him,
Untying thongs to lower sails, then setting
The mast against the mast-rest with the forestays.
505 The men then disembarked on the sea's margin
And dragged the quick ship up onto the dry land,
High up the sand, and laid long stays beside it.
And there they built an altar on the sea-edge
And lit a fire and offered up white barley,
510 And prayed around the altar as he'd ordered.
They took their dinner by the speedy black ship
And poured wine to the blessèd on Olympus.
But when their lust for food and drink was dealt with,
They started off. The lord, the son of Zeus, led,
515 Holding his lovely lyre and playing sweetly,
His steps graceful and high. The Cretans followed
To Pytho, dancing and singing, "Hail, our Healer!"—
The way the Cretan hymnists sing, or pupils
Of the Muse, who touches hearts and throats with sweet tunes.
520 Untiring, they marched toward the crest, and reached
Parnassus and the lovely spot fate granted
To them to live in honored by so many.
His fearful holy precinct and rich temple
He showed them—nonetheless, their hearts were troubled.
525 The captain of the Cretans spoke, inquiring:
"Lord, since you took us from our fathers' country
And all our friends—this must be what you wanted—
How will we live now? Please, explain it to us.
This place has no enticing vines or meadows
530 To let us serve mankind here and still prosper."
Apollo, Zeus's son, smiled as he answered:
"You humans, dismal half-wits, who go looking

517: "Hail, our Healer!"] The Cretans are singing a *paean*, a song in honor
of Apollo in his role as god of healing.

For misery, anxiety, and hardship,
I'll speak in such a way that you remember:
Each of you, with a dagger in his right hand,   535
Can kill sheep endlessly but still have plenty—
Mankind's great tribes will bring to me so many.
So guard my shrine and host the clans of mortals
Who gather here. Above all, show my purpose. . . .
If any word or act of yours is stupid   540
Or criminal—this is the way with humans—
Then other men will come to be your rulers,
And by compulsion you will serve them always.
These are my words: take them to heart and guard them."
So joy to you now, son of Zeus and Leto.   545
I will rehearse your story, then another.

539: One or more lines appear to be missing from the manuscripts in which
this poem is preserved.

4

To Hermes

Muse, sing of Hermes, son of Zeus and Maia,
Lord of Cyllene and flock-rich Arcadia,
The gods' luck-bringing messenger; his mother:
Maia, the bright-haired nymph, and Zeus's lover.
5 She stayed away from where immortals gather,
But in her shadowy cave the son of Cronus
Made love to this well-groomed young thing at nighttime,
While white-armed Hera lay submerged in sweet sleep—
No deathless gods or mortal men could see him.
10 But then, when brilliant Zeus achieved his purpose,
When the ninth moon at last was fixed in heaven,
She brought to light a child worth noticing,
Endowed with wheedling ways, twists, and connivance;
A bandit, cattle-rustler, dream-commander,
15 Gate-lurker, and nocturnal spy, designed
To flash flamboyant deeds among immortals.
Though morning-born, at noon he played the lyre;
He stole the archer's cattle in the evening—
On the fourth, the day the lady Maia had him!
20 He vaulted from his deathless mother's body
But wouldn't settle in his holy cradle.
He jumped from it to find Apollo's cattle.

1: Maia] Hermes's mother is a relatively minor goddess; as a result, Hermes
starts out as something of an outsider among the Olympians.
6: son of Cronus] Zeus.
8: Hera] Zeus's jealous wife.
18: the archer's] Apollo.

38

He crossed the threshold of the high-roofed cavern
And found a lasting source of fun—a tortoise.
Hermes first turned the beast into a singer.   25
Beside the courtyard gates they met each other:
She grazed the flourishing grass outside the house,
Pompously marching. Zeus's son, the helper,
Saw her and laughed and rapidly addressed her:
"A helpful sign so soon! I won't reject you.   30
Welcome, lovely keeper of time for dancing
At banquets. Tortoise living in the mountains,
Where did you get your spotted shell, this nice toy?
Taking you home will sure be worth the trouble.
Just help me out a bit—it's no discredit.   35
Better to go inside and be protected.
Alive, you'll be a wall against bad witchcraft,
But dying you'll make one terrific singer."
That's what he said. He lifted her with both hands
And hauled the tempting trinket from the yard.   40
Upending her, he took a grey iron chisel
And stabbed the life out of the mountain tortoise.
As when someone harassed with swarms of worries
Feels in his mind a thought that swiftly passes,
Or when the eyes send glances spinning out,   45
So noble Hermes planned, pronounced, performed it.
He cut some reeds to measure and secured them
In holes pierced through the beast's shell from the back.
With skill he stretched a cowhide thong around it.
He fitted horns and joined them with a crosspiece,   50
Stretched seven sheep's-gut strings to sound together
Across it. Now he held the fine new gadget
And tried it string by string, hand and pick making

38: one terrific singer] Live tortoises were believed to ward off evil spells;
the dead tortoise's shell becomes the lyre.

Prodigious sounds. He sang along quite nicely—
55 Improvisations such as young boys warble
When at some festival they taunt each other.
He reproduced the intimate discussions
Of Maia (with nice shoes) and Cronian Zeus,
Divulged the splendor of his own conception.
60 He praised the nymph's attendants and her bright house
And all the tripod pots and kettles in it.
But while he sang, his cravings went off elsewhere.
He took the hollow lyre in and concealed it
In his holy cradle. Hot for meat, he darted
65 From the lovely-smelling palace to a lookout.
There he devised some staggering stealth, to rival
Housebreakers in the black hours of the nighttime.
The Sun, driving his chariot and horses,
Went under land toward ocean, and yet Hermes
70 Ran to the shadowed mountains of Pieria,
Since there the blessèd gods' immortal cattle
Were housed, and grazed in fresh and lovely meadows.
Now Maia's son, the watchful Argus-killer,
Cut fifty mooing cows from the holy herd
75 And turned their tracks over the sand and off track.
This is the slick contrivance he arrived at:
He put their front feet where the back ones should be,
Swiveled around, and faced them as he walked.
First, on the beach he crafted wicker sandals—
80 A really wondrous woven innovation,
That mix of tamarisk and myrtle branches.
He tied the flowering brushwood in a bundle
And strapped it snugly underfoot as light shoes,
The leaves still on. The glorious Argus-killer

73: Argus-killer] An epithet of Hermes, derived from one of his later
exploits.

Brilliantly expedited his way home,   85
Plucking his transport in Pieria.
An old man in his flowering vineyard saw him
Go rushing toward the plain through lush Onchestus,
And Maia's splendid son was first to speak:
"Old man with twisted shoulders, scratching at roots,   90
You'll have a lot of wine once grapes are growing. . . .
What your eyes see, don't see. Be deaf while hearing,
And silent: what belongs to you won't suffer."
He spoke, and rushed the hearty cattle onward.
Bright Hermes herded them through shady mountains,   95
Sounding ravines, and plains with floods of flowers.
Then the divine night, which was his dark ally,
Came near its end. Work-bringing dawn was breaking.
Shining Selene, daughter of lord Pallas
The son of Megamedes, climbed her lookout,   100
As Zeus's strong son reached the Alpheus river
Driving Phoebus Apollo's wide-browed cattle.
They came untiring to a high-roofed shelter
And troughs in front of an enchanting meadow.
When he had grazed the lowing cattle richly,   105
He drove them close together to the stable,
Munching on dewy galingale and lotus.
He heaped up logs and engineered a fire,
With a bright branch of laurel he had peeled. . . .
Fitted it in his palm—it breathed a hot blast.   110
So fire sticks and fire were invented.
He placed a load of dry sticks in a deep trench,
Heaving dense armloads there. The fire brightened,
Heat hurtling from the blast of that strong blaze.

91: One or more lines appear to be missing from the manuscripts in which
this poem is preserved.
99: Selene] The moon.

115   Famous Hephaestus flared up high and mighty.
      Now Hermes dragged two bellowing, round-horned bovines
      Up to the fire, with his ample power.
      He thrust the panting animals on their backs,
      Then on their sides, leaned in and pierced their spines.
120   Pressing ahead, he carved out fat-rich pieces,
      Stuck them on wooden skewers and roasted them—
      The meat, the prized back, even the blood puddings
      Stuffed in intestines. All lay on the ground now.
      He stretched the skins across a rugged boulder—
125   Long ages they've remained since they were put there,
      Continually till now. But gleeful Hermes
      Dragged his rich cooking to a smooth, flat rock,
      And out of it he made a dozen portions
      By drawing lots—full honor went with each part.
130   Bright Hermes lusted for the meat he offered.
      The rich smell nettled even an immortal.
      But still that tough and manly heart was stubborn.
      His holy throat would not take what it longed for.
      Instead, he took it to the high-roofed barn—
135   Fat and a heap of meat—and stashed it high up,
      A souvenir. He piled dry wood and fired it,
      Destroying heads and hooves, with no exceptions.
      After the god had finished all these duties,
      He threw his shoes into the deep-whirled Alpheus
140   And quenched the coals and spread sand on the black ash.

115: Hephaestus] God of forging and metalworking, here identified with
the fire he works with.

125: were put there] There may have been rock formations at the site where
Hermes's sacrifice supposedly happened, which were identified with the
hides (line 124).

133: it longed for] Eating meat would make Hermes a human, not one of
the twelve Olympians who simply receive the savor when humans sacrifice
meat to them.

It took all night, but the Moon shone quite nicely.
He dashed back to Cyllene's glittering peaks
At dawn, and met nobody on the long road—
No blessèd god, no human full of dying.
No dogs barked. Hermes, Zeus's son, the "helper,"   145
Squirmed sideways through the keyhole of the hall,
Pliant as fog or wind that blows in autumn.
He snuck straight through the cave to the rich bedroom
On tippy-toes, quite soundless, as if floating.
In haste, heroic Hermes reached his cradle.   150
With muffled shoulders, like a helpless infant,
He lay and fiddled with his knees and blankets—
But in his left hand clutched the gorgeous lyre.
Still, the god couldn't fool his goddess mother:
"Where have you been tonight, you little hustler?   155
Outrageous, how you come home now! I reckon
Leto's son's going to wrap your chest in tight chains
And haul you through our gate. Or random thieving
Will be your lurking life, in the backcountry.
Get out of here. Your father sure made trouble   160
In making you—a pain for gods and humans."
Hermes replied with cunning comments, this way:
"Mother! You snarl like I'm a helpless baby,
Who isn't too experienced in blame—
He's terrified at Mama yelling at him.   165
I'm taking on the very best vocation—
It's going to feed both you and me forever.
We're not just staying here, like you're insisting,
And missing prayers and gifts that other gods get.
Better associate with the immortals   170
From now on—we'll be rich, with lots of wheat fields—
Than sit in this dank cave. And for position:

157: Leto's son's] Apollo's.

The cult Apollo's got—I'm going to share it.
And if my father tells me no, I'll then try
175 To be the king of robbers—'cause I know how.
But if the fabulous son of Leto finds me,
I think it will be even worse for him.
I'll puncture his enormous house at Pylos
And help myself to pots and flashy tripods—
180 And gold, of course, and loads of shiny iron,
And scads of clothes. Just watch me, if you want to."
The son of aegis-holding Zeus and Maia,
The lady, were still talking on this topic
When Dawn the early-born rose from the deep streams
185 Of Ocean, bringing light to men. Apollo
Came to the handsome coppice of Onchestus,
The loud Earth-holder's sacred place. An old man
Pastured his stalwart beast by the vineyard path,
And Leto's glorious son got his attention:
190 "Old man, grassy Onchestus's thorn-plucker,
I come here from Pieria seeking cattle—
All of them are my own herd's curved-horned females.
Alone, apart from these, the black bull foraged;
Four dogs with glittering eyes came after them,
195 Just like a squad of men. But they were left there,
The dogs, the bull as well—it was like magic.
They went away, just as the sun was setting,
From the soft meadow and its luscious grass.
Old-timer, tell me if perhaps you witnessed
200 Anyone on this road behind my cattle."
The old man answered him and spoke as follows:
"Fellow, it's not so easy going over
The things I see. A lot of people pass here—
On crime sprees, or else trying to be decent.
205 They come and go. It's hard to know for each one.
The whole day long until the sun went under,

I've been here digging in my plot of vineyard.
But Sir, I guess I thought I saw a baby—
Someone or other—who had fine-horned cattle.
This newborn with a staff skipped this way, that way.   210
He forced them backward with their heads against him."
Hearing these words, Apollo went on faster,
But saw a slim-winged omen-bird and realized
The robber must be Cronian Zeus's child.
The lord Apollo, son of Zeus, then hurried   215
To holy Pylos for his shambling cattle,
His massive shoulders hidden in a blue cloud.
The archer, when he saw the tracks, exclaimed:
"Hey, what's this supernatural thing I'm seeing?
Footprints—it's got to be—of straight-horned cattle,   220
But turning *back*, into the field of lilies.
And here no man walked, and no woman either—
And no grey wolf, I see, or bear or lion.
And I don't even think a mane-necked centaur
Could take such outsize steps in its swift journey.   225
They span the road—weird, and on this side weirder."
The lord Apollo, son of Zeus, then hurried
Clear to the woody mountain of Cyllene,
To the shadowy den of rock where the divine nymph
Had had a child by Zeus the son of Cronus.   230
A pleasing odor swathed the holy mountain,
And lots of slender-footed sheep grazed on it.
Into the dark cave, over the stone threshold,
Apollo the far-shooter rushed in person.
When Zeus and Maia's son perceived Apollo   235
The archer, furious about his cattle,
He hunched in fragrant blankets, like the deep coals
Of tree stumps huddled in a bed of ashes—
So Hermes squeezed up when he saw the archer.
He squirmed his head and hands and feet together   240

Like a cozy-dozing newborn. But he lay there
Awake and held his lyre in his armpit.
The son of Zeus and Leto recognized them—
The lovely mountain nymph and her dear child,
245 Although he was a stealthily wrapped baby.
Peering in all the corners of the large house,
He took a bright key and unlocked three cupboards
Crammed with lovely ambrosia and nectar.
A heap of gold and silver lay there also,
250 And the nymph's extensive plum and silver wardrobe—
The ordinary blessèd-god provisions.
When he had poked through all the mansion's closets,
The son of Leto spoke to glorious Hermes:
"Hey, baby in your cradle, tell me right now:
255 Where are my cows? Or we could have a bad fight
Soon. I could throw you down the murk of Tartarus,
The awful, endless dark, and Mommy and Daddy
Could never bring you back to daylight. Down there
You'll wander—with the job of lord of babies."
260 But Hermes gave him this conniving answer:
"How can you be so nasty, son of Leto?
You've come here looking for your grazing cattle?
I never saw them, never heard about them.
I couldn't point them out, not if you paid me.
265 I guess I'm just a brawny cattle-rustler!
I wouldn't do this—I've got other interests:
Sleep, for example, suckling my mother's milk,
Blankets around my shoulders, getting warm baths.
I hope nobody finds out why we're fighting.
270 The gods who never die would find amazing
The story of a newborn coming indoors
With cattle from the fields. You're talking crap.

256: Tartarus] The deepest part of the underworld.

Born yesterday, I've got soft feet. The ground's hard.
Want me to swear on Dad's head? That's some swearing.
I promise you I really didn't do it   275
Myself, and didn't see who stole your cattle—
Whatever cattle are: the word's all *I* know."
That's what he said, eyes glimmering intensely,
Eyebrows aflicker, gaze distinctly wobbly—
And gave a long, drawn-out, disdainful whistle.   280
Apollo the far-shooter answered, chuckling:
"You cunning con, I bet you've bored already,
Any number of times, into fine houses.
You've shafted more than one man in this one night,
Sacking their homes unheard—for all your glib talk.   285
You're going to hassle lots of shepherd yokels
In high glens, when you find the means for feeding
Your meat lust: shaggy sheep and herds of cattle.
Come on, unless you want to sleep your last sleep,
Exit your crib, companion of the black night.   290
Among immortals you will have this honor:
To be forever known as king of robbers."
Phoebus Apollo spoke and grabbed the baby.
Hand-hoisted now, the mighty Argus-killer
Pondered his options first, then shot an omen,   295
A reckless message from a hard-worked belly.
Right after this he gave a sneeze. Apollo,
On hearing it, let glorious Hermes drop
And sat in front of him—though keen to leave—
And launched this mocking discourse at the infant: 300
"Don't worry, Zeus and Maia's son in diapers,
I still will find my handsome-headed cattle,
Using these signs and you to lead the way there."
He spoke. Quickly Cyllenian Hermes jumped up

296: belly] A fart.

305   And eagerly set off, but pushed his blankets
      Up to his ears and hunched his body, saying,
      "Where will you take me, meanest god, far-shooter?
      Is it because of cows that you attack me?
      I hope the species gets wiped out. I didn't
310   Steal any cows of yours or see them stolen,
      Whatever cows are—I've just heard about them.
      Let Zeus the son of Cronus judge between us."
      When Leto's shining son and herding Hermes
      Had grilled each other fiercely and distinctly
315   On every point, Apollo showed up truthful. . . .
      Just measure to arrest the thief, bright Hermes.
      The Cyllenian used tricks and crafty speeches,
      Trying to hoodwink silver-bowed Apollo.
      But when he found him equally resourceful,
320   He scurried on his journey down the sand tract—
      The son of Zeus and Leto came behind him.
      Zeus's resplendent sons rushed to Olympus—
      Its fragrant summit and their Cronian father—
      Where scales of justice stood at both gods' service.
325   On snowy-peaked Olympus the immortal
      And ageless met when gold-throned dawn had risen.
      Hermes and silver-bowed Apollo stood there
      Before Zeus on his throne. The god who thunders
      On high addressed these questions to his bright son:
330   "Phoebus! A newborn—in a herald getup?
      That's some rich piece of loot. Where did you get it?
      A crucial issue for the gods in council!"
      Apollo lord far-shooter snapped back at him:
      "Father, what you're about to hear's important—
335   Though you say it's just *me* who likes to raid things.
      I've caught this thieving little thug red-handed—
      After I searched all through Cyllene's mountains.
      He's cocky like no god or man that *I've* seen—

And worse than even all those mortal swindlers.
At night he drove my cattle from their meadow, 340
Made off with them along the thundering seaside
Straight into Pylos, leaving two immense trails—
A master imp's achievement—quite impressive.
The black dust showed, with its opposing footprints,
The cattle walking to the lily meadow. 345
This hellion stepped through sand, outside the roadway,
Not with his hands or feet but some contraption,
Some strange device that dug enormous trenches—
Somebody walked on thin oak logs, it looks like.
As long as he was skittering through the sand, 350
All of his dusty trail was quite apparent.
But when he'd covered the expanse of sand path
And reached hard earth, his traces and the cattle's
Vanished. A mortal man did witness him
Driving a wide-browed cow clan straight to Pylos. 355
But once he'd coolly put them in the fence there,
And straddled acrobatically the road home,
He lay as still as black night in his cradle
In the dark, murky cave. A sharp-eyed eagle
Could not have seen him. But his hands kept rubbing 360
His eyes, as he came up with stuff to pull next.
He even had the gall to tell me straight out:
'I didn't see them, didn't hear about them.
I couldn't turn them in, not if you paid me.'"
Phoebus Apollo sat down when he'd said this, 365
And Hermes told the gods another version,
Expounding to their ruler, son of Cronus.
"Zeus, father, out of me you'll get the true facts—
I'm frank and have no expertise at lying.
He came to our place for his shambling cattle 370
This morning when the sun was barely rising,
With no gods there to supervise or witness.

He mercilessly grilled me, with repeated
Threats of throwing me down gaping Tartarus.
375 His youth is at the height of gloss and spunk,
And I'm a day old—not that he disputes it!
Do *I* look like a big, strong cattle-rustler?
Trust me—you say that you're my own dear father:
By all I hope to own, I drove no cows—home.
380 I didn't cross the threshold, and I mean that.
The Sun and other gods fill me with reverence:
I love you and I fear him. You yourself know
That I'm not guilty. But I'll swear a great oath
By this attractive gate of the immortals—
385 And get him someday for this ruthless probing,
Even though he's stronger. Help me, since I'm little!"
The Cyllenian Argus-killer discoursed, winking;
His blanket was displayed across his forearm.
Well, what a foxy son! Zeus had a good laugh:
390 The cows got such an expert, slick denial.
He told the both of them to work together
To find the beasts. Hermes the guide could lead them,
Cutting out all this nonsense, to wherever
He'd sneaked the sturdy-headed cows. The son
395 Of Cronus ordered. Shining Hermes acted.
The aegis-holder's point was made quite swiftly.
Now Zeus's pair of gorgeous children hurried
To the ford of Alpheus in sandy Pylos.
They reached the fields around the high-roofed stable,
400 Where the farm's stock took refuge in the nighttime.
There Hermes went inside the rocky shelter
And drove the sturdy cattle into daylight.
Leto's son glanced aside and saw the cowhides

396: aegis-holder's] That of Zeus, who is protected by the aegis, a magical
goatskin shield.

On a stark rock and questioned shining Hermes:
"You sneak—how could you skin this bovine duo?   405
You're a helpless newborn! There's just no denying
You'll have amazing strength someday. You haven't
Got far to grow, Cyllenian son of Maia."
He spoke, and twisted sturdy ropes of willow. . . .
Yet on the ground right there these took root quickly   410
Beneath their feet, and, intertwining graftlike,
Slipped over all that wild herd, because Hermes
The burglar-brained connived it. Now Apollo
Stared in amazement. The strong Argus-killer
Looked sideways at the ground with glittering eyes. . . .   415
Feverishly scheming . . . then manipulated
The archer, glorious Leto's son, adroitly,
Tough as he was. The lyre sat on his left hand;
He poised his pick above, then struck at each string.
A stunning sound came out. Phoebus Apollo   420
Laughed with the pleasure poured into his spirit.
Divine noise! Sweet lust seized his listening heart.
Still strumming on his lyre enticingly,
The son of Maia took a confident stand
To Phoebus Apollo's left. His voice began   425
A pretty prelude, following the lyre's cry.
He sang about the deathless gods and dark earth,
How they were born, what portion each was granted.
The first the son of Maia praised was Memory,
The Muses' mother—he was one of hers.   430
Then Zeus's noble child hymned the immortals
Down from the oldest, one's birth, then another's—

409: One or more lines appear to be missing here, and at lines 415 and 416, from the manuscripts in which this poem is preserved.

430: one of hers] Hermes belongs to Memory as a poet, one who both depends on memory and preserves memory.

The lyre laid on his arm duly rehearsed them.
Unbearably Apollo's spirit craved it.
435 These were the fluttering words he aimed at Hermes:
"Cow-slaughtering prankster, busy friend of feasting,
What you've been doing merits fifty cattle.
I think we'll reach a nice accommodation
Shortly. But tell me first, sly son of Maia:
440 Did you, straight from the womb, start working wonders?
Or did some human or immortal give you
This splendid gift and teach you holy singing?
This unfamiliar sound is a divine thing.
Never till now has anybody learned it,
445 Not even the immortals on Olympus —
Only you, swindling son of Zeus and Maia.
What art, what anguish-healing music is this?
Where does it come from? Really, it has three things
At once to choose from: fun, and love, and sweet sleep.
450 I also serve the Muses on Olympus.
Dances they love, and shimmering strains of music,
Lush singing and the flute's alluring cries.
But nothing has enthralled my soul as this does—
However brilliant young men's shows at banquets.
455 Zeus's child, your sweet playing is amazing.
Young as you are, you've got impressive talents.
Sit down then, son, and listen, since I'm older.
You'll have your fame among the deathless deities—
You and your mother. This I'll tell you truly.
460 I swear it by this cornel spear I carry:
I'll give you shining gifts and wealth and glory
Among gods. To the end I won't deceive you."
Hermes replied with calculating comments:
"Far-worker, shrewdly you interrogate me.
465 I don't begrudge you taking up this practice:
Today you'll learn. My attitude toward you

Is really very nice. But you know all this.
You, son of Zeus, sit first among immortals.
You're brave and strong and Zeus the counselor loves you—
Divine prerogative—and gave you bright gifts.   470
Archer, they say you know from Zeus's own mouth
Prophecies and divine ranks—all those rulings.
(Myself, I know from these I'll be a rich boy.)
It's up to you—learn anything you want to.
Since it's for harping that your heart now hankers,   475
Just strum and sing and have a really great time.
It's all on me—but give me credit, pal.
Sing nicely, with a grip on your shrill friend here.
You know the best words and the way to put them.
Don't worry: you can take this into lush feasts,   480
Sweet dances, and magnificent processions,
A thrill for day and night alike. Whoever
Pursues this art with talent and discretion
Will from its voice learn everything to please him.
Just play it lightly, gently, intimately.   485
It dodges dismal work. An ignoramus
Who barges in is going to get an answer
That's nothing but a worthless piece of jangling.
But you can master anything you're keen to.
This is for you, then, Zeus's brilliant son.   490
My calling, archer, will be free-range cattle,
Who'll strip the grass from horsey plains and mountains.
My cows will then get close to bulls in bunches
And give me calves of either sex. However
Competitive you are, don't be so angry."   495
He held the lyre out. Phoebus Apollo took it
And handed back a shining whip to Hermes,
Ordaining herding: Maia's son received it
With glee. He took the lyre in his left hand—
Apollo lord far-worker, Leto's bright son.   500

His pick tried every string. His hand's work sounded
Astonishingly sweet. He sang well with it.
They turned the cows back to the holy meadow,
And Zeus's two extremely handsome children
505 Hurried back up Olympus with its snow caps,
Delighting in the lyre. Zeus in his wisdom
Was pleased and made them friends. The love of Hermes
For Leto's son endures since he bestowed
This charming trinket on the archer god
510 To nestle on his arm for skillful playing.
Hermes himself devised another project,
The crying of the syrinx heard from far off.
The son of Leto made this speech to Hermes:
"Maia's son, guide and prankster, I'm still fearful
515 That you'll steal back the lyre—plus my bent bow.
Zeus has commissioned you to structure trading
Among the rich earth's human population.
But would you give a binding oath, as gods do?
Nod then, or call on Styx, enforcing river:
520 I would be satisfied and very grateful."
The son of Maia, nodding, made a promise
Never again to steal the archer's assets—
And stay away from his fine house. Apollo
The son of Leto swore to keep close friendship
525 And love nobody more among the deathless,
No god, and no man born from Zeus, but always. . . .
"I'll give as well a sign for gods to witness,
Precious and certain in my soul. One more thing:
A splendid staff that governs wealth and luck—
530 Gold, three-leafed, to protect you and accomplish
All lawful words and authorized endeavors
For good (I draw from Zeus's own pronouncements).

512: syrinx] Reed pipe.

To answer, though, Zeus-cherished chum: soothsaying
Is not for you or other gods to study.
It lies in Zeus's mind, and I myself swore,   535
Nodding to holy words and bound forever,
That, barring me, among the ever-living
No one would know of Zeus's shrewd decisions.
My brother with a gold sword, please don't urge me
To tell decrees devised by that wide-seer.   540
I'll hurt one mortal man and help another,
Confusing the pathetic tribes of humans.
My voice will help whoever seeks it guided
By cries and flights of birds of certain omen.
Out of my undeceiving words he'll profit.   545
Whoever, though, believing worthless cawing,
Comes in a stupid quest for my predictions,
And hopes for more than the undying gods know—
I call that trip a waste, save the gifts *I* get.
And this I'm adding, son of splendid Maia   550
And aegis-holding Zeus, god-helping spirit:
There are three virgins, sanctified blood sisters,
Enjoying the swift wings that decorate them.
Over their heads pale barley flour is sprinkled.
Their homes are in the hollow of Parnassus,   555
Far off. They teach divining there—my study
As herd-boy (though my father was indifferent).
From there they flutter out in all directions,
Feeding on honeycomb, to get their work done.
When they're inspired with that greenish honey,   560
They speak the truth enthusiastically,
But if the gods' sweet food is taken from them,
They buzz around in a thick mass of fiction.

550: this] Apollo keeps most prophecy as his own office but grants Hermes
three prophetic bee-nymphs found near Delphi.

These then I grant—enjoy them: make your queries
565 Precise, though. If you choose to teach a mortal,
He'll hear your voice quite often, if he's lucky.
Take the wild, shambling cows too, Maia's son.
Care for the horses and the mules with hard loads. . . .
Lions with bright eyes, boars with glistening teeth,
570 And dogs and sheep—all that the wide earth fosters,
Wild or in herds: Hermes the great will rule them:
And be official messenger to Hades,
Unpaid, but with great power for paying honor."
So: lord Apollo loved the son of Maia
575 Every which way, and Zeus put in his blessing.
Hermes is with us all, with gods and men,
Sometimes a help, but always in the black night
A swindler of the mortal tribes of humans.
This is goodbye now, son of Zeus and Maia.
580 I will recite your hymn and then another.

568: One or more lines appear to be missing from the manuscripts in which
this poem is preserved.

572: messenger to Hades] Hermes escorted the souls of the dead to the
underworld.

5

To Aphrodite

Muse, tell what golden Aphrodite did once,
The Cyprian who fills gods with sweet desire,
And tames the tribes of mortals while she's at it—
And birds that cross the air, and beasts below them.
The lovely-crowned Cytherean possesses   5
All beings that the land and ocean nurture.
But there are three she can't persuade or cheat.
Athena, aegis-bearing Zeus's daughter,
The gray-eyed goddess, doesn't like gold-loaded
Aphrodite but loves the works of Ares—   10
War, battles, skirmishes—and splendid craftwork.
Technical education for the earthbound
Began with her: men made bronze-sculpted chariots,
And in their homes the girls with nice complexions
One by one got their lessons in fine weaving.   15
Neither can laughter-loving Aphrodite
Tame shouting Artemis, with her gold arrows.
She likes her bow, and slaughter in the mountains,
The lyre and dancing, shrieks of jubilation,
Shadowy forests, and a lawful city.   20

2: *Cyprian*] Aphrodite is associated with the island of Cyprus because, depending on the story, she was born there or first came ashore there after being born in the sea.

5: *Cytherean*] Aphrodite has close ties to the island of Cythera, just south of the Greek mainland.

8: *Athena*] Virgin goddess of craftsmanship, strategy, and just warfare.

17: *Artemis*] Virgin goddess of the hunt and wild animals.

Shy Hestia too shuns busy Aphrodite.
This lady was firstborn to cunning Cronus—
And lastborn: Zeus the aegis-holder planned it.
Poseidon and Apollo both pursued her.
25 She was unwilling, stubbornly refused them.
The shining goddess swore a powerful oath
On the head of Zeus, her aegis-holding father,
To stay untouched—and this has had fulfillment.
Zeus gave a glorious gift instead of marriage:
30 The house's central seat and fattest portion,
And shares of reverence in all the gods' shrines,
Since mortals give to her the greatest honor.
So: three were not deluded or persuaded.
No one else gets away from Aphrodite
35 Among the blissful gods and human mortals.
She baffles Zeus—who has such fun with thunder:
The greatest god, unrivaled in his privilege,
And shrewd as well. Whenever she desires,
She breeds him easily with mortal women,
40 Unknown to Hera, both his wife and sister,
By far the loveliest eternal goddess,
And grandest born to Rhea and sly Cronus;
And Zeus, whose thoughts are never going to perish,
Has made her his respected, careful consort.
45 Now Zeus gave his tormentor sweet desire
For a human lover, since it was his purpose
To stamp out her immunity to mortals
And stop her ever bragging up in heaven—

21: Hestia] Virgin goddess of the hearth.
23: planned it] Cronus felt threatened by his children and swallowed them
when they were born. Zeus escaped this fate and tricked Cronus into spit-
ting the others out again in a kind of second birth. As the oldest, Hestia was
first in and last out.

With a sweet smirk, because she loves a good joke—
How she combined the gods with death-prone women   50
(Who then gave mortal sons to the immortals)
And goddesses with perishable lovers.
And so he made her hanker for Anchises.
Among the many springs of Ida's tall peaks
He herded cows in all his godlike beauty.   55
When humorous Aphrodite got her first look,
She fell in love—her mind was gone completely.
The Cyprian shrine at Paphos, full of incense,
Features her holy ground and fragrant altar.
She went there, went inside, and shut the bright doors.   60
And there the Graces bathed her and rubbed on her
A holy oil that blooms on the undying—
She kept this heavenly-sweet perfume handy.
Now dressed in every kind of gorgeous garment
And gold-festooned, fun-loving Aphrodite   65
Left fragrant Cyprus—straight to Troy she headed.
High in the clouds she made a speedy journey
To Ida (rich in springs, mother of wild things)
And walked across the mountain to the shelter.
A rush of bears and fast, deer-gobbling leopards,   70
Gray wolves, and bright-eyed lions fawned around her.
She had a look at these and found them charming.
She tossed some lust to make the whole assortment
Pair off and do it in the shadowy coverts.
But on she went and reached the well-built shanties   75
At the camp and found Anchises on his own there,
A hero with god-derived good looks. The others
Were out escorting cows through grassy pastures—
All of them. They had left him by himself there.
He paced and played a shrill tune on his lyre.   80

53: *Anchises*] A prince of Troy, despite his cowherding.

Zeus's child Aphrodite faced him, looking
Like a virgin whom no man had overcome yet—
She didn't want to scare him when he saw her.
Anchises looked her over in amazement:
85   So tall, well-built, and radiantly dressed!—
The robe more brilliant than a flash of fire,
Coiled brooches and bright earrings shaped like flowers.
Around her delicate neck was lovely jewelry
Of gold, ornately worked. As the moon glimmers,
90   So her young bosom marvelously glimmered.
Love grabbed Anchises, and he said to her:
"Hello, my goddess guest! You *are* a goddess?
Artemis? Leto? Golden Aphrodite?
Gray-eyed Athena? Themis full of glory?
95   One of the Graces, maybe, the companions
Of gods in general? Graces too are gods.
Perhaps a nymph, out of some pretty woods,
Or one who lives right here on this nice mountain
With all its stream-heads and its grassy meadows?
100   Where everyone can see, up on a summit,
I'll build an altar, and in every season
Give you good offerings. But you be helpful.
Make me a man that all the Trojans look to,
With children doing great. Give me a long life
105   In the Sun's light, for everything it's worth.
Let me get old and rich among these people."
And Aphrodite, Zeus's daughter, answered:
"Anchises, awesome among earthborn people,
I'm not a god! Why do you say I'm like one?
110   I'm going to die. My mother is a woman.
Otreus is my really famous father—
You've heard about the king of well-built Phrygia?
Oh, but I know your language too—no, really.
My nurse back in the palace was a Trojan.

Since I was little she and not my mother   115
Took care of me. You see: I know your language.
Just now the gold-staffed Argus-killer snatched me
Out of the festival of loud, gold-arrowed
Artemis. Lots of girls just right for marriage
And brides danced in the middle of a big crowd.   120
The Argus-killer with his gold wand took me
And flew me over lots of people's farmland,
And lots of unworked ground that has no owners.
(Animals hunt there in the shady places.)
I'm off the fertile earth for good, I thought then—   125
But the god said I'd sleep with you, Anchises,
And that I'd be your wife and have great children.
And when the burly Argus-killer told me,
Explained it all, he went back to the families
Of gods. I came to you. I have to be here.   130
I ask by Zeus now and your classy parents
(I see from you that they're not trashy people):
Before you've done it, while I'm still a virgin,
Take me to meet your father and your mother
(Who knows what's right) and all their other children.   135
I'll make a good relation, not a bad one.
Send right now to the hurricane-horsed Phrygians,
To tell my father and my worried mother.
They'll send you lots of gold, and woven clothes too.
All this good stuff will make a massive dowry.   140
Then celebrate our marriage with a dinner
That deathless gods or people won't look down on."
The goddess spoke, inspiring sweet desire.
Love seized him, and he spoke out and addressed her:
"You're human? And your mother is a woman?   145
And Otreus—the famous—is your father?

117: Argus-killer] Hermes.

Hermes the holy messenger has brought you
To me—and you'll be called my wife from now on?
Well, nobody, no god or human being
150   Is going to stop me making love to you
Right now—even if silver-bowed Apollo,
Aiming from way off, shoots his painful arrows.
You look just like a goddess. I'd be willing
To live with Hades once I've been in your bed."
155   He took her hand. The laughter-loving goddess
First shied away and looked down with her sweet eyes,
Then stole into the well-made bed. Soft blankets
Lay on it for the hero, and above them
Were skins of bears and deep-voiced lions slaughtered
160   By the young man himself on towering mountains.
The two got on the well-constructed bedstead.
But first he took the shining costume off her—
Pins, spiral brooches, necklaces, and earrings—
Undid the belt and stripped her shimmering clothes
165   And draped them on a chair with silver rivets,
Then—it was fate, and the gods' will—Anchises,
A man, badly informed, slept with a goddess.
But as the shepherds brought their cows and fat sheep
Back to the shelter out of flowering fields,
170   The goddess poured sweet sleep over Anchises
And decked herself again in gorgeous clothes.
Now well and thoroughly redecorated,
The shining one stood by the bed, head brushing
The well-made roof. Her cheeks flashed superhuman
175   Loveliness—just like the bright-crowned Aphrodite's!
She roused him from his sleep now, saying this:
"Up, sleepyhead, Dardanus's descendant,
And figure out if this was my appearance

154: To live with Hades] To die.

In front of you when I had just arrived here."
She spoke. He hastily obeyed and woke. 180
Seeing the neck and eyes of Aphrodite,
He promptly turned his terrified gaze elsewhere,
Ducking his fine face underneath the blanket—
But sent winged words at her in supplication:
"Goddess, the moment that I laid eyes on you, 185
I knew you were divine. You were a liar.
I ask you now, by Zeus who holds the aegis,
Don't leave me impotent for my whole lifetime.
Have pity, since you know a man does badly
After he's slept with an immortal goddess." 190
Then Zeus's daughter Aphrodite answered,
"Anchises, best among these death-prone humans,
Cheer up, and get a handle on your terror,
Since I'm not going to hurt you, and the other
Gods also won't— you're lucky that we like you. 195
You're going to have a son, lord of the Trojans
(And he'll have sons, and they will—it keeps going).
His name will be Aeneas, for my anguish
In stumbling into bed with you, a mortal.
Your family, though, among all mortal people, 200
Are closest to the gods in their appearance.
The counselor Zeus kidnapped blond Ganymede,
In fact, to bring his beauty into heaven.
He now pours drinks for gods in Zeus's mansion,
And everyone admires his stunning beauty, 205
As he takes red nectar from a golden bowl.
But Tros was inconsolable, not knowing

198: anguish] The name of Aeneas is here connected to the Greek word
ainos, meaning "grievous."
202: Ganymede] A mortal youth who became Zeus's cupbearer; son of
Tros, who was also Anchises's great-grandfather.

Where the amazing storm had whisked his dear son.
Day after day he went on howling for him.
210 And Zeus felt bad and gave him compensation:
High-stepping horses, transport for immortals.
He gave this gift to keep and sent the killer
Of Argus as a messenger to tell him
His son would be like gods, ageless and deathless.
215 As soon as Zeus's word came to the father,
He mourned no longer; all his thoughts were happy.
With glee he rode behind the storm-legged horses.
Dawn of the gold throne made off with Tithonus—
A relative of yours, like the immortals.
220 She went to ask the black-cloud son of Cronus
To stop his death and let him live forever.
Zeus nodded to her, gave her what she longed for.
But Lady Dawn, the idiot, neglected
To ask for youth, the molting off of old age.
225 As long as his delicious bloom stayed with him,
He had his fun with gold-throned, early-born Dawn
And lived at lands' end by the streams of Ocean.
When finally gray hairs trickled into sight
Out of that handsome chin and scalp of his,
230 The lady Dawn steered clear of sleeping with him—
But kept him in her palace, caring for him,
Supplying first-rate clothes, food, and ambrosia.
When hateful old age got a really good hold,
Pinned him and kept his arms and legs from moving,
235 She thought it over carefully and then chose.
She put him in a room and shut the bright doors.
His voice runs pitifully, although no power
Remains, these days, in limbs that were so springy.

238: that were so springy] These lines imply what is explicit in other versions: in his withered state, Tithonus has become a cicada.

Among the gods that's not the way I'd have you:
I would prefer you not to be immortal.   240
If, as you are—with just these looks and body—
You lasted and were known to be my husband,
No grief would overwhelm my clever brain.
But as things are, soon ruthless age will wrap you;
It does present itself to every mortal: 245
Destructive pest—the gods themselves just hate it.
Among the deathless gods I'll be embarrassed
My whole eternal life, since I was with you.
My tricks and sweet talk got them all: immortals
Forced to be intimate with mortal women—   250
They lived in fearful slavery to my whims.
But now my mouth had better never open
To mention this in heaven. I went crazy—
Terribly: left my mind somewhere behind me,
Slept with a man—beneath my belt's a baby.   255
Him: from the moment that he sees the sunlight,
Deep-bosomed mountain nymphs will bring him up.
They live here in this high and holy mountain,
And don't quite rank with mortals or immortals.
Their lives are long. The food they eat is holy.   260
And with the gods they dance enticingly.
The Sileni and the sharp-eyed Argus-killer
Get friendly with them deep in pleasant caves.
For each one born, an oak tree, with a high head,
Or fir grows in the ground that feeds young manhood: 265
High mountains grow luxuriant with their beauty.
Towering they stand, and they are called the precincts
Of the immortals. Humans will not cut them
With steel. But when a nymph's death stands beside her,

262: Sileni] Wild, half-animal companions of nymphs and the god
Dionysus.

270 Then in the ground her pretty tree first withers.
     The bark goes rotten, and the twigs start falling,
     And the two souls leave the Sun's light together.
     These nymphs will keep my son with them and raise him.
     And when he gets to be a gorgeous young man,
275 The goddesses will bring him here to show you.
     But just to let you know what I myself plan:
     In four more years I'll come and bring him with me.
     And when you have a chance to see your child,
     You'll be so pleased, since he'll be heavenly-looking.
280 Then take him right away to windy Ilion,
     And if some human mortal ever asks you
     What mother had your dear son in her belly,
     Remember and just tell him what I tell you:
     'It was some pretty nymph—or that's what I heard.
285 They live here in this forest-covered mountain.'
     If you get stupid, though, and brag and tell them
     How you made love to rich-crowned Aphrodite,
     The angry, smoldering bolt of Zeus will hit you.
     That's all. Make sure you keep it to yourself now.
290 Don't say my name, but think of the gods' anger."
     Thus winding up, she dashed to windy heaven.
     Joy, goddess ruling over well-built Cyprus.
     I've made a start with you. Now here's another.

280: Ilion] Another name for Troy, Anchises's home.

6

To Aphrodite

I'll sing of gold-crowned, lovely Aphrodite,
Honored owner of Cyprian battlements
Set in the sea, where the wet-gusting west wind
And the soft-foaming, racketing waves bestowed her.
On shore the Hours in their gold headdresses   5
Met her with joy, draped her in sacred clothes,
And crowned her deathless head with intricate gold;
And in her ears, already pierced, went earrings:
Flowers of precious gold and mountain-copper.
They hung her tender neck and silvery breasts   10
With necklaces of gold, just like the Hours wear
Themselves when in gold diadems they visit
Their Father's house to join enticing dances.
Once they had thoroughly adorned her body,
They took her to the gods, who made her welcome,   15
Each with a hand clasp, each with prayers to take her
Home as his lawful wife: they were amazed
By the beauty of the violet-crowned Cytherean.
Joy, sexy-glancing darling. In this contest,
Give me the victory. Make my hymn ready—   20
The first for you, another in the future.

2: *Cyprian*] Aphrodite is associated with the island of Cyprus where, as told
here, she came to land after being born from the sea.
18: *Cytherean*] Aphrodite has close ties to the island of Cythera, just south
of the Greek mainland.

7

To Dionysus

I'll sing the son of glorious Semele,
Dionysus, standing on the barren sea's edge,
On a jutting height and looking like a young boy
In his first bloom, his lovely black hair flowing,
5 A purple cloak resting on his strong shoulders.
There soon approached a ship with sturdy benches—
Bad fortune brought Etruscan pirates near
Over the wine-dark sea, and when they saw him,
They nudged each other, rushed ashore, and caught him.
10 They threw him in their boat, gleefully thinking
He was the son of heaven-nurtured rulers.
They set about to tie him with their hard ropes.
Willow twine jumped away and would not hold him.
He simply sat there, with a simper lurking
15 In his black eyes. And when the helmsman saw,
Immediately he called to his companions:
"Idiots! Who's this strong god that you're trying
To tie up? But the sturdy ship can't hold him!
He may be Zeus, or silver-bowed Apollo,
20 Or else Poseidon—he's not like a mortal,
But rather like those living on Olympus.
Come on, let's let him loose on the black land—
Quickly, since if you touch him he'll be angry
And raise hard winds and giant storms against us."
25 He spoke, but was berated by the captain:
"Look for a good wind, fool, secure the ropes
And raise the sail. This boy will be men's business.
I think he'll find his way to Egypt—Cyprus—

Or Hyperboria, or even farther.
He'll point us in the end to his connections 30
And tell us what he's worth. God sent him our way."
That's what he said to get the mast and sail raised.
The sailors stretched the ropes, the canvas bellied.
Right then, amazing things began to happen.
First, a delicious, fragrant wine went gurgling 35
Over the fast, black ship, transcendent odors
Rose, and the sailor witnesses were staggered.
Along the sail's top edge a vine extended:
Bunches of grapes were dangling thickly from it.
Around the mast black ivy wound itself, 40
Covered with blossoms and enticing berries.
Garlands festooned the oarlocks. Seeing all this,
They gave belated orders to the helmsman
To bring the ship to land, but now the god changed
To a savage, bellowing lion on the prow. 45
A shaggy bear amidship was the next sign.
It reared in frenzy. From his height the lion
Burningly glared to rout the sailors sternward.
In fear they stood around the sober helmsman.
The lion did not hesitate to pounce. 50
He took the captain, sent the sailors leaping
Into the bright sea to escape a dark fate.
They became dolphins. Pitying the helmsman,
He held him back and blessed him, saying these words:
"Don't be afraid, since my heart knows your value. . . . 55
I am roaring Dionysus, and my mother
Is Zeus's lover Semele, child of Cadmus."
Joy to you, lovely woman's son, since no one
Forgetting you can put sweet song in order.

8

To Ares

Gold-helmeted, strong Ares, chariot-mounted,
Hard in your will, hand, shield, and spear; bronze-armored,
Staunch city saver, bulwark of Olympus,
Father of Victory, helper of Themis,
5   Tyrant to enemies, leader of good men,
King over manliness! Your fiery globe whirls
Among the seven planets' tracks, your horses
Blazing forever over the third orbit.
Hear me, ally of mortals, maker of fine youth:
10 Rain gently from on high into my being
Brightness and martial strength. Let me have power
To shake out of my head the bitter panic,
Defeating with my mind my soul's false impulse,
And yet keep down the temper that provokes me
15 Toward icy strife. But, blessèd god, give courage—
The kind that lives in peace among the mild laws,
Away from combat and death's savage demons.

1: Ares] As a war god, Ares is often associated with bloodshed and savagery, in contrast to Athena, goddess of just warfare. Here, in a hymn in his honor, he is presented more positively.

4: Themis] Goddess associated with order and justice.

9

To Artemis

Sing, Muse, of Artemis, the archer's sister,
The arrow-raining girl raised with Apollo.
Her horses drink in Meles with its deep reeds.
Her pure gold chariot speeds its way through Smyrna
To viny Claros. Silver-bowed Apollo   5
Sits waiting for the long-range arrow-pourer.
To you and other goddesses, I sing this:
Be joyful. It is you that I begin with,
But after you another hymn must follow.

10

To Aphrodite

I sing the Cyprus-born Cytherean, giver
Of luscious gifts to mortals. Her sweet face
Smiles at them always. On her cheeks sex blossoms.
Joy to you, ruler of sturdy Salamis
5   And Cypress in the sea. Make my song charming.
First I will sing your hymn, and then another.

11

To Athena

I come now to the fearsome town-defender,
Pallas Athena. She and Ares foster
Campaigns, the battle cry, the sack of strongholds.
The people come and go in her protection.
Joy, goddess! Grant me wealth, grant me good fortune.   5

12

To Hera

Hera I sing, the gold-throned child of Rhea,
Supremely beautiful, her reign unending,
Sister and noble wife of thundering Zeus.
All of the blissful gods on high Olympus
5   Venerate her, with Zeus who loves the thunder.

13

To Demeter

Demeter I begin, dread, bright-haired goddess—
Persephone also, her exquisite daughter.
Joy, goddess! Guard this city, lead my anthem.

14

To the Mother of the Gods

The mother of gods and mortals—sing her, Muse,
Daughter of powerful Zeus, with your clear voice.
Drums, castanets roar for her pleasure, flutes cry,
Lions and wolves with bright eyes howl and bellow.
5 Echoing mountains, shaded streambeds charm her.
You my song greets—and all the goddesses.

1: mother of gods and mortals] This could be Demeter, or Rhea, mother of
the Olympians, but the drums and castanets suggest Cybele, an Asiatic god-
dess also worshiped by the Greeks.

15

To Lion-hearted Heracles

Heracles I'll sing, the Zeus-born best of mortals.
Alcmene, who was cloud-dark Zeus's lover,
Gave birth to him in Thebes with its fine plazas.
Over the endless earth and sea he wandered
At first, at lord Eurystheus's orders.   5
Violence he often brought and often suffered.
Snowy Olympus is his lovely home now.
He lives in joy with Youth, slim-ankled consort.
Goodbye, lord, Zeus's son: grant skill and riches.

1: Heracles] Heracles is one of the few mortals to become a god, entering
Olympus and marrying Hebe, or Youth.
5: Eurystheus's] Before he could become a god, Heracles had to atone for
a series of violent acts by performing twelve labors for the Argive king
Eurystheus.

16

To Asclepius

I launch Asclepius the healer's anthem.
Shining Coronis, daughter of King Phlegyas,
On the Dotian flatlands gave him to Apollo.
He soothes our agonies and brings us gladness.
5   Bliss to you, sovereign whom I pray to, singing.

1: Asclepius] A mortal healer, son of Apollo and the mortal woman Coronis, who became a god associated with medicine.

17

To the Dioscuri

Muse, sweetly sing of Castor and Polydeuces,
Whom Zeus above made stepsons of Tyndareus.
High on Taÿgetus lady Leda had them:
The black-cloud son of Cronus had seduced her.
Joy, Tyndareans, riders of fast horses!   5

1: *Castor and Polydeuces*] Twin "Dioscuri," or sons of Zeus, born when
Zeus mated with Leda, wife of Tyndareus. Helen and Clytemnestra were
also born form this union, although some accounts make Clytemnestra and
Castor wholly mortal, the children of Tyndareus, not Zeus.

18

To Hermes

Hermes the Cyllenian Argus-killer,
Flock-rich Arcadia and Cyllene's ruler,
Quick messenger of gods and son of Maia
(Atlas's modest child, Zeus's seduction)!
5   She shunned the blissful crowd of the immortals.
At night the son of Cronus used to mate with
The pretty-haired nymph in her shadowy cave
While white-armed Hera lay possessed by sweet sleep:
No men or ever-living gods could see him.
10   I make you welcome, Zeus and Maia's offspring.
I'll start with you then step along in singing,
Joy-giving messenger and blessing-bringer.

19

To Pan

Muse, tell me of the cherished son of Hermes,
Goat-hoofed, goat-horned, glad uproar: Pan, who ranges
With dance-delighted nymphs through groves and fields.
They walk the mountains—goats do not go higher—
Calling on Pan, the glistening-haired herd-god,   5
Grown muddy ruling over snowy ridges
And mountain peaks and roadways strewn with boulders.
He wanders here and there in crowding thickets,
Once in a while enticed toward tender rivers,
And sometimes rambling in the stony highlands.   10
He climbs the peaks—the flocks show in the distance.
Often he lopes along the gleaming massifs,
Or chases wild things on the lower ridges,
Sharp-eyed for prey. But finally at evening
He shouts, returning from the hunt and piping   15
Sweet tunes. A bird among the leaves and blossoms
Of spring is not more skillful with her sad songs,
Pouring out notes however honey-throated.
Swift-stepping mountain nymphs with their clear voices
Perform with him beside a spring's black water.   20
The echo's moan circles the mountain summit.
The god goes back and forth and to the middle
And leads them with his stamping. A lynx's pelt
Lies tawny on his back. The high songs thrill him
In the soft meadow with its random blossoms   25
Of crocus and sweet-smelling hyacinth.
They sing the blessèd gods on high Olympus,
Especially how Hermes, speedy helper

And ready messenger of the divine ones,
30 Came to Arcadia, rich in sheep and wellheads—
The place of the Cyllenian's holy precinct.
The god was shepherd of a curly flock there
For a mortal, since the sap of soft desire
Rose in him for the sleek-haired child of Dryops.
35 The marriage blossomed. In his house she gave him
A darling son whose face was strange to look at—
A horned, goat-footed bellower and laugher.
His nurse jolted away and fled her young charge—
Terrified of the fierce, full-bearded vision.
40 Luck-bringing Hermes took him in his own hands
And overflowed with joy in his divine heart.
He hurried to the gods' homes with his baby
Wrapped in a hare's thick skin from off the mountains.
By Zeus and all the other gods he placed him,
45 Showed them his son: then all of the immortals
Were glad—most of all Bacchic Dionysus.
They called him Pan, since bliss was his pandemic.
Joy, lord, and let this anthem bring me favor
As from this record of you I go onward.

46: Bacchic Dionysus] Dionysus, like Pan, is especially associated with animals, wild places, and revelry.

47: pandemic] Pan's name is here connected with the Greek word *pan*, meaning "all."

20

To Hephaestus

Shrill Muse, sing of Hephaestus, great inventor.
He and gray-eyed Athena taught all bright works
To mortals on the earth, who made their poor homes,
Like animals, in caverns in the mountains.
But now Hephaestus, glorious in his knowledge,   5
Has made them skilled. They spend the seasons' circle
In peace and comfort now, in their own houses.
Hephaestus, lend your grace: teach and reward me.

21

To Apollo

Beside the eddying Peneus descending,
The swan's voice and her wingbeats shrill you, Phoebus.
With his heart-piercing lyre the singer chants you:
You are the first and last of all his sweet words.
5   Joy, lord, and may my music win you over.

22

To Poseidon

I start to hymn the splendid god Poseidon—
Sea lord, shaker of land and barren water,
Master of Helicon and spacious Aegae.
Earth-rattler, heaven gave you two commissions:
Deliverer of ships, breaker of horses.   5
Joy, earth-surrounder with your blue hair streaming!
Holy one, be compassionate to sailors.

23

To Zeus

Zeus I will hymn, the greatest and the noblest,
Wide-seer, king, fulfiller, who converses
Closely with Themis as she leans in toward him.
Matchless, world-watching Cronian, be gracious.

24

To Hestia

Hestia, keeper of the lord far-shooter
Apollo's holy house in splendid Pytho;
With smooth anointment flowing through your hair:
Come to this house, draw near it, with like-minded,
Shrewd Zeus, and lend your favor to my singing.   5

25

To the Muses and Apollo

I now strike up the Muses, Zeus, Apollo.
Apollo the far-shooter and the Muses
Have given earth its singers and its harpers—
And Zeus its kings. A man the Muses cherish
5   Prospers. A voice flows from his mouth like honey.
Joy, Zeus's children! Honor what I sing you.
I'll tell your story, then another after.

26

To Dionysus

This is for ivy-crowned, loud Dionysus,
Glorious Semele and Zeus's bright son.
Sleek-haired nymphs took him from his kingly father
Into their arms—devoted foster mothers
In Nysa's hollows. As his parent wished it,   5
He grew, the gods' peer, in a fragrant grotto—
They raised him so the world could sing his glory.
Later, festooned with laurel leaves and ivy,
He wandered forest places, and the nymphs came
Behind him, while the endless woods reechoed.   10
Welcome now, Dionysus, with your grape-wealth.
Bring us in joy to see this season next year,
And to the years to come in their abundance.

27

To Artemis

Artemis I sing, gold-weaponed, shouting hunter;
Shy, arrow-raining virgin, shooter of stags,
The sister of Apollo of the gold sword.
On shadowy mountain slopes and windy summits
5   She loves to stretch her pure gold bow in hunting,
Sending out painful arrows. The peaks tremble
High overhead. The shady forest bellows
Terribly with the deaths in it. Earth shudders,
Shudders the fish-full sea as, warrior-hearted,
10   She massacres wild beasts on every side.
But when the keen-eyed arrow-pourer's had
Her fill of fun, then she unstrings her bent bow.
She comes to wealthy Delphi, to the great house
Of Phoebus, her dear brother, where she guides
15   The sweet steps of the Muses and the Graces.
She hangs her arrows and her arching bow up,
And, covered now in lovely clothes and jewelry,
She leads the dance, from which immortal voices
Hymn pretty-ankled Leto, whose two children
20   Are best among the gods in thought and action.
Joy, Zeus and beautiful-haired Leto's children.
First I will sing of you, and then sing onward.

28

To Athena

The gray-eyed Pallas rises from my singing,
Noble and shrewd and with a heart of iron,
Revered, courageous, city-saving virgin,
Born at Tritonis out of the holy skull
Of Zeus the counselor and dressed in armor   5
Of brilliant gold. Awe seized the gods who saw it.
From the divine head of the aegis-holder,
From Zeus's forehead in a rush she vaulted,
Shaking her sharp spear. Great Olympus spun
Frighteningly from the gray-eyed young girl's power.   10
The earth around her screeched, the sea was shaken
To froth of purple waves, but soon it halted.
Hyperion's bright son stopped his rushing horses
The whole long time it took the girl to strip off
The god-size armor from her holy shoulders: 15
This was Pallas Athena, joy of wise Zeus.
Goodbye then, child of Zeus who holds the aegis.
You I will tell about, and then another.

13: *Hyperion's bright son*] The Sun.

29

To Hestia

Hestia, all the high-built homes of mortals,
Who walk the earth, and of the deathless gods,
Grant you an everlasting seat, fine portion
And right, and greatest honor. In your absence
5   There are no mortal banquets. You are offered
A honey-sweet libation first and last.
Come, Zeus and Maia's son, Argus-destroyer,
Luck-bringer, messenger with your gold staff,
Live with her in this bright house, in close friendship. . . .
10 Join with sweet, modest Hestia and help us:
Be generous—you both know earth's heroics;
Come aid the minds and muscles of earth's people.
Cronus's daughter, joy!—and gold-wand Hermes.
I will recite your hymn and then another.

7: *Zeus and Maia's son*] Hermes, who is Hestia's perfect complement, because he is always traveling and crossing boundaries, while she never leaves the hearth.

30

To Earth, Mother of All Things

I'll sing of Earth, life's mother, the rock-founded
Oldest god, and the feeder of creation.
Whatever walks bright land, whatever paddles
The sea or flies—your wealth alone provides for.
You give lush fields and lovely children, lady.   5
You give and take the livelihood of humans.
Whoever your heart honors with its kindness
Is happy—all things lavishly are his.
Crops weigh his fields down, cattle crowd his meadows,
And fine possessions overflow his mansion.   10
Earth's favorites rule by good laws over cities
Of lovely women; splendid wealth attends them.
Their sons thrive in exuberance and pleasure.
Their joyful virgin daughters leap and scamper
In flower-draped troupes on softly blooming meadows.   15
This is your favor, holy, generous goddess.
Joy, mother of gods, and starry Heaven's consort.
Give me a heartening living, for my song's sake.
I'll sing another song when yours is over.

2: *feeder of creation*] Hesiod's account of the origins of the universe, the
Theogony, begins with Gaia, the Earth, who starts the generations of the
gods by creating Uranus, or Heaven, and making him her consort.

31

To Helios

Sing Helios, Muse, Zeus-born Kalliope!
This god was Earth and starry Heaven's grandson;
Bright son of gentle-eyed Euryphaëssa.
Hyperion married his own famous sister,
5 Euryphaëssa, and they had fine children:
Rosy-armed Dawn, Selene with her bright hair,
And the godly-beautiful, untiring Sun,
Who shines both for the dying and the deathless,
Driving his horses. Terribly his eyes glare
10 From his gold helmet, and his body flowers
With dazzling rays, while bright hair from his temples
Half-covers handsome and far-beaming features.
His weightless-woven, splendid clothing flickers
At the wind's breath. The stallions pull him forward . . .
15 And halts the gold-yoked chariot and horses,
Until the marvelous seaward ride through heaven.
Goodbye, lord. Please, give me a happy living!
I start with you, but earthly half-gods follow:
I'll praise the acts the gods let mortals witness.

1: Helios] The Sun.
6: Selene] The Moon.
14: One or more lines appear to be missing from the manuscripts in which
this poem is preserved.

32

To Selene

You, mistresses of music, sweet-voiced daughters
Of Cronian Zeus, teach me the fine-winged Moon's hymn.
Straight down from her undying face in heaven
Her beams roll over earth. Great beauty rises
And radiates. Air that was lightless glitters.   5
Rays from her gold crown linger all around.
She bathes her pretty body in the ocean
And dresses in far-shining clothes. Selene
The brilliant yokes her bright, neck-arching, fine-maned
Horses, and hurries on her evening journey.   10
Her great, month-splitting orbit now is finished;
Her beams are most resplendent in her fullness—
A guide and signal from the sky for mortals.
Zeus gave to her his love and bed and body,
And she conceived her little girl, Pandeia—   15
Even among the gods a brilliant beauty.
Joy, rich-haired, white-armed, noble, bright Selene!
Be kind to me. I'll move from you to heroes,
To works of half-gods made well-known by singers,
Those pleasure-speaking henchmen of the Muses.   20

33

To the Dioscuri

Coy Muses, tell of Zeus's shining children,
Tyndarean sons of slender-ankled Leda:
Horse-tamer Castor, blameless Polydeuces.
She joined in love with Zeus of the black cloud,
5   Then under Taÿgetus's towering reaches
She gave them birth: the saviors of earth's people
And rapid-running ships when gusts of winter
Batter across ungentle seas. The sailors
Pray for the help of powerful Zeus's sons
10   And kill white lambs for them high on the stern deck.
Enormous winds and crescents of the water
Engulf the ship till, suddenly, the gods come,
Dashing with shrilling wings from the high heavens.
Quickly they tame the blasting of the hard gale
15   And smooth the waves down on the foam-strewn surface—
Salvation's miracle. The sailors see it
And with elation stop their bitter labor.
Goodbye, Tyndareans, riders of fast horses.
This song is yours: another one comes after.

34

To Guest-friends*

Respect a stranger's need for house and hosting
In your steep town where Hera's sweet-faced nymph lives,
High-summited Saedene's lowest foothill.
You drink the tawny river's holy water:
Immortal Zeus's child, bright-flowing Hermus.   5

---

*To Guest-friends] This hymn does not appear in all manuscripts of the collection and is addressed not to a god, but to guest-friends. Guest-friends were acquaintances who provided hospitality to travelers, a sacred duty protected by the gods.

2: steep town] Cyme, on the west coast of present-day Turkey.

Glossary of Names

(First occurrence in the text noted by hymn and line number.)

Aeneas: Son of Aphrodite and Anchises. A Trojan leader in the Trojan War, later said to be founder of Rome. 5.198

Aidoneus: Another name for Hades. 2.2

Amphitrite: A sea-goddess, wife of Poseidon. 3.94

Anchises: A prince of Troy and father of Aeneas by Aphrodite. 5.53

Aphrodite: Goddess of love and beauty. Married unwillingly to Hephaestus, she had many affairs, most notably with Ares and the mortals Adonis and Anchises. 2.102

Apollo: God of the bow, music, prophecy, sudden death, plague, and medicine. Patron god of the Delphic oracle. Twin bother of Artemis. 3.1

Ares: God of war. Son of Zeus and Hera. Lover of Aphrodite. 3.197

Argus-killer: Epithet for Hermes, who killed Argus, a man with many eyes, while Argus was guarding Io for Hera. 3.197

Artemis: Virgin goddess of hunting and childbirth. Twin sister of Apollo. 2.424

Asclepius: A mortal healer, son of Apollo and the mortal woman Coronis. Became a god associated with medicine. 16.1

Athena: Virgin goddess of craftsmanship, strategy, and just warfare. Favorite child of Zeus. She sprang fully-grown from his head. 3.308

Castor: See Dioscuri. 17.1

Celeus: Father of Demophoön. King of Eleusis. 2.96

Claros: Oracle of Apollo in the city of Colophon on the coast of Asia Minor. 3.40

Cnossos: A town on Crete. Political and ceremonial center of Minoan culture 3.393

Crete: The largest of the Greek islands in the Mediterranean, southeast of Greece, home of Minoan civilization. 2.124

Cronian: Son of Cronus. 1.13

Cronus: Youngest Titan, son of Earth and Heaven, husband of his sister Rhea, and father of Hestia, Demeter, Hades, Hera, Poseidon, and Zeus. 2.21

Dawn, the: A goddess, the personification of the dawn, named Eos. 4.184

Delos: A small island in the Cyclades between Greece and Asia Minor. Birthplace of Apollo. 3.16

Delphi: Site of Apollo's oracle, on the mainland north of the Gulf of Corinth. 27.13

Demeter: Goddess of fertility and agriculture, also known as Deo. Mother of Persephone. 2.1

Demophoön: Son of Celeus and Metaneira. 2.233

Deo: Another name for Demeter. 2.47

Dione: A Titan and mother of Aphrodite. 3.93

Dionysus: God of wine and madness, son of Zeus and a mortal woman, Semele. 1.20

Dioscuri: The twin sons of Zeus, Castor and Polydeuces, born when Zeus mated with Leda, wife of Tyndareus. 17.0

Earth: Named Gaia, the first being after Chaos. Mother of the Titans by Heaven. 3.84

Eileithyia: Goddess of childbirth, who helps women in labor. 3.97

Eleusis: Town near Athens and site of the Eleusinian Mysteries of Demeter 2.97

Erebus: A primordial god, the personification of darkness. Sometimes used as an epithet for Hades. Also considered the boundary between the living world and the underworld that the dead had to pass immediately after dying. 2.335

Europe: The part of mainland Greece north of the Gulf of Corinth, as opposed to the Peloponnesus, which is the large peninsula to the south. 3.251

Eurystheus: Argive king for whom Heracles was forced by Hera to perform twelve heroic labors. 15.5

far-shooter: An epithet for Apollo. 3.1

far-worker: An epithet for Apollo. 3.56

Hades: God of the underworld, also known as Aidoneus. Brother of Zeus and Poseidon. 2.79

Harmony: A goddess named Harmonia, daughter of Ares and Aphrodite. Wife of Cadmus, the king of Thebes. 3.195

Heaven: Father of the Titans, named Uranus, personification of the sky, son and consort of Earth. 30.1

Hecate: A helpful, mediating goddess, later associated with witchcraft. 2.24

Helios: The Sun. Apollo is sometimes identified as Helios. 2.61

Hephaestus: God of forging and metalworking. Married to Aphrodite. The only disfigured god, Hephaestus is lame, the result of either his birth or being thrown from Olympus by Hera. 3.317

Hera: Goddess, wife and sister of Zeus. The patron goddess of marriage. Jealous of Zeus's many lovers, she sought revenge from them or their children. 1.7

Heracles: Son of Zeus and a mortal, Alcmene. His gift was tremendous strength. Hera forced him to complete twelve difficult labors. He eventually became a god. 15.1

Hermes: God of boundaries and transgression, known for his cunning and shrewdness. He is a messenger of the gods. 2.340

Hestia: Virgin goddess of the hearth and domestic life. 5.21

Hours, the: Goddesses of time and seasons named the Horai. 3.194

Hyperion: A Titan and father of Helios the Sun. The name Hyperion is often used as an epithet for Helios. 2.26

Iambe: Eleusinian servant who jokes with Demeter and lifts her spirits. 2.195

Ilion: Another name for Troy. 5.280

Inopus: River running through Delos. 3.18

Iris: Messenger of the gods. 2.314

Leto: Mother of Apollo and Artemis by Zeus. 3.5

Maia: A shy nymph who lived on Mount Cyllene. Mother of Hermes by Zeus. 4.1

maenad: An ecstatic female worshiper of Dionysus. 2.386

Metaneira: Mother of Demophoön. Queen of Eleusis. 2.162

Muses: Nine goddesses from whom poets, thinkers, and artists derive their inspiration. 3.189

Naxos: Island in the Cyclades south of Delos, birthplace of Dionysus and place where Theseus abandoned Ariadne. 1.3

Olympus: Highest mountain in Greece, location of the throne of Zeus and residence of the gods. 1.15

Ortygia: Sometimes an alternate name for Delos, but here another island. 3.16

Pallas: An epithet for Athena. Athena accidentally killed Pallas, a Titan, and ever after wore his goatskin, fringed with serpents, as her protective aegis. 2.424

Pan: God of shepherds, with goat horns and legs, who plays pipes and dances with nymphs. 19.2

Parnassus: Mountain where Delphi is located, on the mainland north of the Gulf of Corinth. 3.269

Peloponnesus: Peninsula comprising southern Greece, connected to the north by the slender Isthmus of Corinth. 3.250

Persephone: Goddess of the underworld, daughter of Demeter and Zeus. Hades kidnapped and married her. 2.55

Phoebus: "Shining," one of Apollo's most common epithets. 3.20

Pieria: Region in the southern part of Macedonia. Home of the Muses. Mount Olympus, the home of the ancient Greek gods, is located on the southern border of Pieria. 3.216

Polydeuces: See Dioscuri. 17.1

Poseidon: God of the sea and of horses. Brother of Zeus and Hades. 3.230

Pytho: Another name for Delphi. Either named after the snake, Pytho, which Apollo killed at Delphi, or the source of the snake's name. The name of the snake is connected to the Greek verb *puthô*, meaning "to rot." 3.183

Rhea: Wife of Cronus. Mother of Hestia, Demeter, Hades, Hera, Poseidon, and Zeus. 2.60

Selene: The Moon. Artemis is sometimes identified as Selene. 4.99

Semele: Daughter of Cadmus, king of Thebes, and Harmony. Mother of Dionysus by Zeus. 1.4

Sileni: Wild, half-animal companions of nymphs and the god Dionysus. 5.262

Styx: River in Tartarus upon which the gods take oaths. Also the river the dead must cross to enter Hades. Often personified as a goddess, the daughter of Erebus. 2.259

Tartarus: The deepest part of the underworld, often the personification of the underworld. 3.336

Taÿgetus: Mountain separating Laconia, the Spartan homeland, from Messenia to the west. 17.3

Telphusa: Both a spring near Delphi and the nymph associated with it. 3.244

Themis: Goddess associated with order and justice. 3.94

Thetis: A powerful sea-goddess. Mother of Achilles. 3.319

Titans: Twelve godlike giants, the children of Uranus and Gaia. Cronus and Rhea, the king and queen of the Titans, were the parents of the first Olympian gods. After defeating the Titans in battle, Zeus imprisoned them in Tartarus, the deepest part of the underworld. 3.335

Tithonus: Brother of Priam. Dawn's lover. 5.218

Tros: Father of Ganymede and king of Troy. 5.207

Troy: City in the northwest of Asia Minor, site of the Trojan War. 5.66

Tyndareus: Father of the Dioscuri. King of Sparta. 17.2

Typhaon: A monster with a hundred fiery snake heads that spoke with human and animal voices. Son of Earth by Tartarus. Fought with Zeus but was eventually defeated. 3.306

Victory: Daughter of Ares, known as Nike. 8.4

Wealth: Another name for Hades. 2.489

Youth: A goddess named Hebe, daughter of Zeus and Hera. Wife of Heracles after he became a god. 3.196

Zeus: Ruler of the gods, son of Rhea and Cronus. Zeus and his brothers divided the earth between them: Zeus gained control over the heavens, Poseidon the sea, and Hades the underworld. Married to Hera, Zeus took many lovers and fathered many children. 1.4

Selected Bibliography

Allen, Thomas W., ed. *Homeri Opera Tomus V Hymnos Cyclum Fragmenta Margiten Batrachomyomachiam Vitas Continens.* Oxford: Clarendon Press, 1912.

Allen, Thomas W., W. Reginald Halliday, and E. E. Sikes, eds. *The Homeric Hymns*, 2nd ed. Oxford: Clarendon Press, 1936.

Athanassakis, Apostolos N. *The Homeric Hymns: Translation, Introduction, and Notes.* Baltimore: Johns Hopkins University Press, 1976.

Chapman, George, trans. *Homer's Batrachomyomachia, Hymns, and Epigrams*, 2nd ed. London: J. R. Smith, 1888.

Clay, Jenny Strauss. *The Politics of Olympus: Form and Meaning in the Major Homeric Hymns.* Princeton, NJ: Princeton University Press, 1989.

Crudden, Michael. *The Homeric Hymns.* New York: Oxford University Press, 2001.

Foley, Helene P. *The Homeric Hymn to Demeter: Translation, Commentary, and Interpretive Essays.* Princeton, NJ: Princeton University Press, 1994.

Fröhder, Dorothea. *Die dichterische Form der Homerischen Hymnen.* New York: Ohms, 1994.

Janko, Richard. *Homer, Hesiod, and the Hymns.* New York: Cambridge University Press, 1982.

Lombardo, Stanley, trans. *Hesiod: Works and Days and Theogony.* Indianapolis: Hackett Publishing Company, 1993.

Miller, Andrew M. *From Delos to Delphi: A Literary Study of the Homeric Hymn to Apollo.* Leiden: E. J. Brill, 1986.

Pearcy, Lee T. *The Shorter Homeric Hymns.* Bryn Mawr, PA: Thomas Library, Bryn Mawr College, 1989.

Radermacher, L. *Der homerische Hermeshymnus erläutert and untersucht.* Vienna: Hölder-Pichler-Tempsky, 1931.

Richardson, N. J. *The Homeric Hymn to Demeter.* Oxford: Clarendon Press, 1974.

Sargent, Thelma. *The Homeric Hymns: A Verse Translation.* New York: W. W. Norton, 1973.

Shelmerdine, Susan. *The Homeric Hymns.* Newburyport, MA: Focus Classical Library, 1995.

Steiner, George, ed. *Homer in English.* New York: Penguin, 1996.

West, Martin L., ed. and trans. *Homeric Hymns, Homeric Apocrypha, Lives of Homer.* Cambridge, MA: Loeb Classical Library, 2003.